Cretan
Cuisine

The best traditional Recipes for Health and Longevity

Contents

Introduction

History

The Mediterranean diet is currently considered by Nutritionists as a modus vivende that endows people with longevity and sound health, with Crete at its epicentre, as supported by research conducted on an international scale1. It was established that the inhabitants of Crete manifest the lowest mortality indices with respect to cardiovascular diseases and cancer. Researchers then focused their attention on the particular aspects of nutrition responsible for such robust health.

The history of Cretan diet is very old; its roots lie deep in the Neolithic Age. Today science has no proof, only circumstantial evidence of the dietary habits of Cretans 5,000 years ago. However, a clear picture of those habits emerges from as far back as 4,000 years ago, when the Minoan civilization was at its peak. On the basis of archaeological findings, it seems that ancient Cretans, the Minoans, consumed pretty much the same products that are being consumed by modern Cretans today. Large clay jars (pithoi) were found in Minoan palaces that were used for the storage of olive oil, grain, legumes, and honey. In various pictorial representations2 we can also see the magnificent world of Cretan plants and herbs.

During the Byzantine period, the Cretans remained faithful to their dietary legacy and cooking habits. On the one hand, urban families were keen on preparing elaborate meals distinguished for their exceptional taste. On the other hand, the rural population subsisted strictly on products grown: greens, fruit, legumes, olives and olive oil. The Cretans, however, applied their accumulated knowledge and imagination to these lowly products producing delicious results. This practice sustained Cretans through adverse times, in periods of successive occupation by the Arabs (824-961), the Venetians (1204-1669) and the Turks (1669-1898). A turning point in the Cretan diet occurred with the introduction of new crops, particularly of the tomato, from the New World

The conquerors came and went from Crete, but the Cretan spirit, religion, language and cuisine remained unchanged over the centuries!

Products

For Cretans, the secret of longevity is very simple. They eat anything that their rich soil produces! They consume a lot of fruit, vegetables, greens, fresh produce, legumes, cheese and bread. Cretans use herbs to add flavour to their meals; they make sweets/cakes with natural sweeteners, honey and grape-juice syrup; while the excellent Cretan wine is an indispensable accompaniment to their meals. Cretans do not eat meat or, rather, they did not eat meat until a few decades ago. Meat has always had a ritual quality in Crete, and generally in Greece. In modern times, they consumed meat only a few times a year, i.e. during festivities or, if wealthy enough, every Sunday. The ingenuity of Cretans exploited fully the entire spectrum of ingredient combinations, which resulted in volumes of recipes for meals and deserts.

Teaching Health & Culture

Modern Cretans feel the urge to share their secrets of life with the world. Besides their history and culture, they are also willing to share with people their prized cultural heritage known as CRETAN DIET. Cretans would like to let the world know of a gigantic effort taking place on the island to preserve traditional values and nutritional customs, in spite of the influx of promotional activities favouring foreign nutritional habits, mainly that of fast food. Cretan producers and local processing, packaging, and marketing companies warrant that all Cretan products are pure, without chemical substances or other preservatives and additives. Cretan products, being part of a centuries old tradition, are treated with the same respect as that afforded to them by our ancestors.

Organic Farming

The natural environment of Crete favours the development "earth friendly" methods of growing crops, particularly with regard to basic agricultural products, i.e. those that have adjusted well to the climate of Crete. In the last few years a group of organic

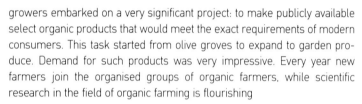

Table 1: Death rates recorded in cohort groups in a period of 15 years after the commencement of the Seven Countries Study.

PER 100.000 SUBJECTS	CORONARY	CANCER	OVERALL MORTALITY
Finnland	972	613	2169
USA	773	384	1575
Zutphen (the Netherlands)	636	781	1825
Italy	462	622	1874
Former Yugoslavia	242	394	1712
Corfu (Greece)	202	338	1317
Japan	136	623	1766
Crete (Greece)	38	317	855

Table 2: Death rates from coronary heart disease and overall mortality per 100,000 subjects.

	SEVEN COUNTRIES STUDY (10 YEARS)		WORLD HEALTH ORGANIZATION (1987)	
	CORONARY HEART DISEASE	OVERALL MORTALITY	CORONARY HEART DISEASE	OVERALL MORTALITY
Finnland	466	1390	386	1210
USA	424	961	263	1061
The Netherlands	317	1134	224	1016
Italy	200	1092	148	1066
Former Yugoslavia	145	1021	137	1302
Corfu (Greece)	149	847	123	932
Japan	61	1200	53	837
Crete (Greece)	9	627	7	564

growers embarked on a very significant project: to make publicly available select organic products that would meet the exact requirements of modern consumers. This task started from olive groves to expand to garden produce. Demand for such products was very impressive. Every year new farmers join the organised groups of organic farmers, while scientific research in the field of organic farming is flourishing

Olive Oil

By the end of 1950's, when American nutrition experts came to Crete to investigate the causes that were responsible for the longevity of Cretans, they could not believe their eyes! "My God, how much oil do you use!," exclaimed Dr. Ancel Keys, as he was looking at a plate of green salad virtually floating in olive oil. In fact, Dr. A Keys' observation was subsequent to similar remarks/observations made centuries earlier by travellers from other regions of the world, who were also interested in scrutinizing the daily life and habits of Cretans.

Today it is believed that the secret for a long and healthy life lies in olive oil, the principal ingredient of Cretan diet. Past and present research conducted in the USA and Europe supports the view that olive oil not only shields the human heart from diseases, but also increases the good operation of other organs or protects the human organism from a long range of diseases. For one thing, it reduces cholesterol3; it has excellent antioxidant properties and wards off all forms of cancer; in addition, it supports the operation of liver and is ideal for those people suffering from diabetes and other diseases!

Table 2 was compiled on the basis of the 10-year results from the Seven Countries Study and the statistical data released by WHO in 1987

The quality of Cretan and Aegean olive oil enjoys wide reputation all over the world. This is because it is not an industrial but a natural product received by crushing the olive fruit and is free from preservatives and chemical additives. It is pure, light and tasteful; in short, it is the best olive oil in the world. The olive trees are cultivated with love and care, with due respect for tradition, while the juice is packaged pure by small packaging units that respect themselves and their consumers.

Try pure olive oil instead of butter in your breakfast ... just dip country hardbread, or a slice of whole-kernel bread in it! You may find this an excellent and tasteful alternative to your normal breakfast. Olive oil can be flavoured by mixing it in the bottle with a combination of herbs or those of your choice.

Introduction

Aromatic Plants

Another important Cretan tradition. Ancient authors (e.g. Aristotle) recorded the following observation: a wild goat wounded by a hunter's arrow would try to find a certain plant, origanum dictamus L., the king of the endemic flora of Crete. As soon as the wild goat consumed this plant, the arrow would fall off the wound by itself! In antiquity dictamus was considered a form of panacea (cure-all natural medicine). Hippocrates, for example, recommended dictamus that facilitated labour and delivery in pregnant women. Cretan pickerf of aromatic herbs offer a wide variety of products as oregano (origanum onites), basil (ocimum basilicum L.), tilia cordata mill., marjoram (origanum majorana), thyme (thymus sibthorpil benth.), mint (mentha), rosemary (rosmarius officinalis), bay (laurus nobilis L.), camomile (matricaria chamomilla L.), sage (salvia officinalis), a.o. All these herbs have been used as medicinal plants since antiquity and numerous texts by ancient authors attribute to them excellent therapeutic properties. Many of these Cretan herbs (among them dictamus) grow on steep slopes on the island and are usually gathered by experienced people. Today these herbs are used for tea preparations and as a condiment; they can be found in most local markets and supermarkets. The herbs are dried under natural conditions and then packaged by modern packaging units without any form of chemical processing.

Introduction

Wines

Cretans are very well aware of the health benefits from moderate wine consumption; it is part of their culture: good wine is a perfect accompaniment to every dinner but should be taken moderately. Consumption of wine is not a solitary practice; it goes hand in hand with social events, good company and comradeship.

Modern wine industries of Crete have exploited the traditional grape varieties and the centuries old accumulated knowledge of wine-making. The oldest wine-press found on Crete, in the village of Archanes, is 3500 years old. In this sector, also, tradition is in harmony with technological progress. Cretan wine makers combine traditional ways with modern technology and marketing strategies. Qualified enologists experiment with succulent grape varieties to produces wines that are distinguished for their bouquet and taste that satisfy a wide range of consumer demands. The Cretan "appellation d'origine" ("designation of origin") wines constitute an invaluable heritage of traditional selections absolutely harmonized with the climatic conditions of the island. Let us not forget that viniculture is a 4000 year old practice on the island of Crete. In Greek mythology, wine was the present of a great god, Dionysus, to the people. Dionysus is the god of wine-making and merry-making, life and friendship. According to mythology, Dionysus' favourite companion was Ariadne, the daughter of Minos, king of Crete. Dionysus . . . wine . .the Minoan civilization . . .nutrition as a way of life... these are concepts intricately woven in the fabric that constitutes our culture. Areas distinguished for their wine varieties: Archanes, Peza (province of Pediada), Dafnes, Monofatsi, Province of Siteia, Province of Kydonia and Kissamos.

Tsikoudia (Or Raki)

It is a limpid, alcoholic drink that is mainly made of the "strafila" (the grapes' peel, after the wine has been produced). There is also a tsikoudia made of berries (mournoraki), which is particularly alcoholic, with a strong flavour and taste. It has been known since the Turkish domination, it is served in special, very small glasses and is usually served with peanuts. The arrival of the refugees from Asia Minor changed this typical snack into apakia, siglina, matured peppery gruyere, snails with rosemary and wine (hohli boubouristi) etc.

Tsikoudia can be found in all the coffee shops, food-shops, restaurants, even in the "in" cafes of Crete and of course in all the houses. You can buy both bottled and unbottled tsikoudia. You can also find it in many of Athens' food-shops.

Introduction

Fruits

That which distinguishes the Cretan diet from any other type of Mediterranean diet is the significantly higher requirements for fruit consumption. It has been estimated (A Keys, 1970 and D. Kromhout, 1989) that the average Cretan consumes four times more fruit than the average southern European and six times more than the northern European (e.g. the average Dutch).

Oranges are typical winter crops widely produced in various parts of Crete. 19th century travellers on Crete extolled their rich taste and large consumption. When oranges are in season, they are purchased in large quantities by families and are consumed raw or squeezed for juice. Oranges are particularly rich in vitamin C, while vitamin B12 is distinguished for its hematopoietic action, and vitamins A, C and E for their antioxidant properties. That which distinguishes the Cretan diet from any other type of Mediterranean diet is the significantly higher requirements for fruit consumption. It has been estimated (A Keys, 1970 and D. Kromhout, 1989) that the average Cretan consumes four times more fruit than the average southern European and six times more than the northern European (e.g. the average Dutch). Oranges are typical winter crops widely produced in various parts of Crete. 19th century travellers on Crete extolled their rich taste and large consumption. When oranges are in season, they are purchased in large quantities by families and are consumed raw or squeezed for juice. Oranges are particularly rich in vitamin C, while vitamin B12 is distinguished for its hematopoietic action, and vitamins A, C and E for their antioxidant properties.

Again, tradition plays a major role in the cultivation of citrus crops. The trees are completely adjusted to the temperate climate of the island and produce fruit of excellent taste. Processing units (mainly for orange and citrus juice) are modern with methods that balance harmoniously international standards and tradition. Grapes are the par excellence fruit of the summer season and considered ideal for a balanced diet. As mentioned earlier, the antioxidant elements contained in their skin protect against cancer while other trace elements are indispensable for the good operation of the human body. The grapes grown on Crete are distinguished from those grown elsewhere in the Mediterranean for their excellent aroma and taste. In recent years we have witnessed the extensive cultivation of special traditional varieties, which are free from pips and, therefore, can safely be consumed even by little children. Greek mythology says that Gaea (the goddess of earth) gave Zeus and Hera citrus fruit as wedding presents. These presents were guarded in the Garden of Hesperides, far from the inquisitive eyes of mortals. Today, citrus crops are cultivated widely in the province of Chania, while others can be found in the valley of Messara, at Fodele (Heraklion area), at Mylopotamos, and elsewhere.

Raisins - Dried Fruits

In Crete, raisins and must, along with honey, constitute the most important traditional sweeteners. Viticulture on Crete dates from prehistoric times. Raisin production is an ingenious way to preserve in dehydrated (dry) form a product that thrives in the long summer season. The vines of Crete produce ideal varieties of grapes that can easily by turned into raisins. The drying of grapes is a natural process, under the hot summer sun. Since Cretans consume significant amounts of raisins, they also reap the benefits of their rich in vitamins content (A B1, B2, B3, B6, etc.). Raisins are consumed either raw or mixed in various other preparations, e.g. cakes, rolls, pies, or in combination with dried fruits. These delicious pastries and bakery products contain the minimum in fatty substances and no cholesterol.

Dried fruits are one more favourite source of food for Cretans. They are rich in linoleum and linoleic acid and thus a perfect shield for the heart. The dried fruits of Crete come from trees, which receive no form of care or cultivation! Walnut trees, chestnut trees and almond trees are not systematically cultivated! Ohey grow and bear fruit as they have been doing for centuries now! Their fruit is absolutely natural and free from chemical substances, thus complying fully with the Cretan prototype of nutrition.

Honey

One of the most important exhibits in the Archaeological Museum of Heraklion, a museum that houses most of the secrets of the famous Minoan civilization, is an exquisite gold piece of jewellery representing two bees flanking a round portion of honeycomb. This exhibit is the most eloquent witness of the relationship between Cretans and bees. It is the same copper-coloured bee-mentioned by ancient authors - whose delicious, velvety product befits the dinner table of gods; the bee that nested inside the sacred cave, the birthplace of Zeus. Honey, this exceptionally natural sweetener, contains precious substances and can be consumed even by people suffering from diabetes! It is also rich in vitamins and anti-oxidants. Vitamin E, the basic vitamin in honey, along with other substances, removes harmful substances from the body that either originate from the body itself or are the result of human activities, e.g. smoking, radiation, and consumption of processed food that is usually incriminated for tumour growths. The honey of Crete is completely natural and is produced in regions of endemic vegetation. The bio-system of Crete is rich in endemic plants, particularly herbs. This vegetation and herbs are the favourite source of food for bees. A tour of the bee-keeping areas of Crete is enough for visitors to understand why Crete produces the most aromatic honey in the world: the beehives are amidst a variegated landscape scented by aromatic bushes and herbs, most of them endemic to Crete. Since snow covers only the highest mountain peaks, albeit for a few months a year, and owing to the protracted summer season, wild vegetation is always available to bees for foraging. Crete has produced honey since pre-historic times! -- without interruption, as if nothing had changed. Perhaps the structure of the beehive improved, but all else must have remained unchanged: the bees, the aromatic herbs, the environment. Processing of the Cretan honey is by natural methods, without high temperatures that destroy the vitamins.

Introduction

Garden Produces

One more basic feature of the Cretan diet is the large consumption of vegetables and other products of vegetable origin. On average, Cretans are at the top of the scale in terms of vegetable consumption. In fact, they consume three times the amount of vegetables than Europeans! That, too, is part of their secret for a long and healthy life. This dietary habit provides the average Cretan with an abundance of fibers, vitamins, and other nutrients required for human sustenance.

At the same time vegetables contain trace elements many of which are essential in metabolism or for the production of essential compounds, while deficiency in those elements causes metabolic syndromes. Vegetables promote the good operation of the intestines and ward off cancer of the large intestine. Their contribution to the operation of the digestive system is remarkable, and they are rich in vitamins necessary for the metabolism of various tissues. Much of the vegetables consumed in large quantities on Crete are rich in fatty acids which prevent cardiac diseases and most forms of cancer.

The linoleic acid contained in the variety of vegetables consumed by Cretans is a true shield of health! It protects the heart and the circulatory system. Some of the most common garden produce of Crete originates from other regions of the world, e.g. the tomato, which revolutionized the Cretan cuisine and shaped the character of Cretan diet as we know it today.

Cretan tomatoes are naturally ripened and free from hormones. Other agricultural products of Crete, cucumbers, marrows, etc., are cultivated in the lush valleys of the island under the most favourable weather conditions -- no snow during winter and moderate temperatures at the heart of the summer.

Areas that are considered most favourable for vegetable production are mainly found in the south of the island, in niches where even the swallows do not need to migrate further south, to Africa. The garden produce of Crete grows in a natural environment, under the moderate temperatures of a slanting golden sun and within a naturally scented environment. Cretans have a particular affection for the soil that provides them with the means for a good, long life. Technology is good as long as it does not violate and debase their dietary codes the observance of which gave Cretans the title of the lowest heart-attack risk, the lowest death rate, and the greatest life expectancy in the Western world.

Garden produce is cultivated in the southern, coastal regions of Crete, mainly at Ierapetra, Messara, south of Rethymnon, in the coastal area of Selino, of Kissamo and elsewhere.

Cheese - Olives - Rusk

Cheese

Cheese consumption on Crete is the largest on a world scale! Cretans do not actually see food as some sort of medicine; they know how to enjoy different tastes. The taste of Cretan cheese, gruyere and its varieties (kefalotyri, kefalograviera), sweet and sour soft cheese and other dairy products is unsurpassed! A significant source of calcium and proteins with high biological value, the Cretan cheese plays a significant role in Cretan diet. It is said that cheese is a source of saturated fat, but Cretans who eat a lot of cheese are not found with high levels of cholesterol. This is probably due to a balanced diet, which prevents the building up of harmful substances in the human organism. Indeed, the Cretan dietary prototype provides an impressive balance of nutritive elements that are precisely those required by the human body to remain healthy.

Recent scientific research correlated the effects of protein break-down in the dairy products with the prevention, treatment, and evolution of tumour growths in the breast and prostate! Currently, there is extensive research going on in Crete and France to develop new methods for the treatment of such tumours on the basis of related scientific results!

Milk is rich in vitamins A, B1, B2, B3, B6, pholic acid, basic minerals and amino-acids. The activities of goat- and sheep-raising on Crete are deeply rooted in myth. It is said that the dairy products of Crete provided nourishment to the great god, Zeus, who was born in a cave on the island and nursed by a goat, Amaltheia. Since then, the character of goat- and sheep-raising on Crete has seen but little changes. Stock-raising is only in terms of small animals, goats and sheep, that roam free in the scented pastures of the island. There are no organised stock-raising units and all animals feed on the wild plants and herbs.

This traditional form of stock-raising exploits traditional knowledge accumulated throughout the centuries. The only difference is that milk processing does not take place inside or outside sheepfolds any more, but in modern processing units which balance traditional forms of processing with approved standards of hygiene. The Cretan gruyere is exceptional in taste, as it is the case with other types of local cheese.

Anthotiros
(or *sweet* / *fresh* mizithra)

It is produced solely from fresh sheep or goats' milk. It is a very good, slightly soft, sweet white cheese, with a very soft taste and compact texture, in the shape of a cone, without skin and holes. It is very low in fat, therefore it is very healthy. A table cheese that you can eat either as an appetiser or with your food. It is a fine dessert, since it can also be eaten with honey.

Dry Anthotiros
(or *dry* mizithra)

It is made by drying the fresh anthotiros (it is salted in the drying process), that is why it is a more piquant cheese, of whitish colour and compact texture, in the shape of a sphere or a cone, without skin and holes. It is a fine cheese that can be eaten plain but also grated, with spaghetti. It can be used to make an excellent ladotiri (oil-cheese- you cut it in pieces and store it in oil).

Sour Mizithra
(local name -Xinomizithra)

This soft, creamy, white cheese with its granular texture has a slightly sour taste. It is produced from sheep
or goat's milk or a combination of both. The ideal sour
mizithra is made of goat's milk. It is a fine cheese, tasty
and rich at the same time, without skin and holes.
Both types of mizithra are eaten in many ways: plain,
spread on bread, with dried rusk (dacos), in the salad,
as a filling in cheese patties, Kalitsounia, pies, etc.

Pichtogalo
from Chania
(former name: soft mizithra)

It is made from sheep or goat milk or a combination
of both. The best Pichtogalo is made from goat milk. It
is a fine soft, white cheese, very light, with a light sour-
ish, fresh and pleasant taste, without skin and holes.

Kefalograviera
(local name) - (Small traditional Cretan gruyere)

It has exactly the same appearance as gruyere. It is
made from sheep milk or a combination of sheep and
goat milk. It has a more vivid colour than gruyere and
its' taste is piquant, full and slightly salted. Kefalograviera is part of the tradition of western Crete, since
its' production at the Chania prefecture has started many
years now. Ideal when served as a table cheese.

Cretan Gruyere
(local name)

It is a hard cheese, of yellow colour, with natural hard greyish skin, smooth soft texture and small holes. It is produces solely from fresh Cretan sheep milk. It has a discreet flavour and soft taste it is slightly salted and its' taste holds the flavour of fresh bread, butter, milk and roasted dried fruits. While the "old gruyere" (matured for 12 months) has a piquant taste and a more intense flavour.

Malaka
(or Tiromalaka or Tiromalama)

It is a fresh cheese (cheese mass) and it is used only for filling Kalitsounia or pies. It is produced from fresh Cretan goat and sheep milk.

Ladotiri
(cheese in oil)

A very mature, old cheese (over a year) and quite dehydrated. It can be made using gruyere, kefalograviera or dry anthotiros. The cheese is cut in pieces and completely covered with virgin olive oil. This is a very old way of processing cheese, which obviously has its' origins both in the most difficult financial conditions of the older days and the lack of technical means for preservation.
You can buy ladotiri in selected shops that sell Cheese-dairy products in Chania.

Cheese

Traditional yoghurt

It is made of high quality fresh sheep's milk, and of course due to its' freshness, all of the milk's fat is transferred to it. However, this is also the reason why it is very tasty, with a soft milky fresh taste and light flavour. Many producers of the Chania Prefecture sell their yoghurt, both in Dairy product shops and supermarket chain stores.

Stakovoutiro
Butter made from Staka

It is produced by cooking the milk's cream. In the past it was only prepared in the households, but nowadays it is sold in all the grocery stores and in Chania's Municipal Market. It has a whitish or yellowish colour, rich in fat, with a milky tang and a special flavour that makes roast meat extremely tasty. It is mainly used when roasting meat but you can also use it when cooking pilaff (sizzle a small quantity and pour it over the rice). Use small quantities in order for the food not to be too greasy.

Staka
(anthogalo)

It is the cream of the milk. It is the first product that is produced when processing milk (by beating it, we make fresh butter) and of course it is very rich in fat. It can be eaten plain, raw- spread on bread or fried- accompanying other dishes, mainly meat, or with fried eggs (a first -class dish!).

Olives

Salted black olives, seliniotikes or alatsolies

Take small black olives, wash and soak them in water for 3 days. Then take a straw basket, put a layer of ground salt it, then put a layer of olives and continue until you have reached 25 cm below the basket's surface. Shake the basket every 5-6 days in order for the olives to mix and be salted well. 18 to 20 days later, put them in a strainer, sift them in order to remove the salt, wash, strain and oil them with your hands and they are ready to be served.

Pickled olives

Take big black olives and carve them, using a razor (when doing so, see not to carve them to the stone). Put them in a big bowl filled with water and leave them for 5-6 days, changing the water every morning and evening. Then put them in a big vase filled with water, where you have added a very small amount of lime (use a pat of lime, the size of a nut, for 10 kg of olives) and soak for 4-5 hours. Afterwards soak them in vinegar for one day, strain them and put them in a vase filled with oil, where they can be preserved for a long time.

Green olives, crushed

Take big green olives (tsounates), wash them and crush them with a flat stone, taking care not to break their stones. Put the olives in a big saucepan, add hot water and leave them for ½ hour this will keep their colour bright. Strain them, put them in big glass vases or earthenware vases and add water. Change the water every morning and evening for 5-6 days to soak out their bitterness (if needed, leave them for 1-2 more days).
Dissolve some salt in a glass of water *, add some lemon or sour orange juice and add the mixture in the vase. Add some oil too (a layer of oil, 1 cm thick, should be formed on the vase's surface). This way, the air will not come to contact with the olives and this will prevent mould formation.
* The ingredients make a 5 kg vase.

Bread and Rusk

Crete is a mountainous island and its' economy was mainly dependant on stockbreeding and agriculture. The lifestyle of the Cretan people was hard, yet fully adapted to the island's geological and financial framework. Therefore, the general conditions, the products available on the island and the geological difficulties combined created special nutritional habits, adapted both to the daily needs and the potentials of the island's residents. One of these habits, probably the most characteristic all over Crete, is the rusk (dried bread), which was created due to the need, of stock-breeders in particular, to eat bread that would be kept in good condition and be tasty and nutritional at the same time. Therefore, the Cretan rusk became an inseparable friend for all those who had to be away from home for a long time. Due to its' particularly good taste and great variety, which was created with time, the rusk is always found on the Cretan table, next to the bread, and has taken up a special place in all the social and festive functions of the island's residents. There are many varieties of rusks with common characteristics: the ingredients (cereals); their dry, hard, harsh texture; the fact that they are extremely tasty and easy to digest, and above all, their origin to which they owe their name: "Cretan rusk".

You can find the following rusks: those called horiatika and eftazima, the barley, wheaten and rye rusks, the sweet small rusks and the very special "boukies" (bite size) with their pleasant, neutral taste - a fine sweet, ideal for accompanying tea and coffee.

A first-class Cretan rusk is the rusk called Eftazimo, which is made from chickpeas and wheaten flour. It also contains salt, pepper, red peppers and bay leaves. It has a very special, pleasant taste, its' colour is light yellow and you can find it in various sizes, the most common being the square. It is a traditional product exclusively made in Crete, it is considered to be a formal type of bread and is offered at weddings and important celebrations

Wedding Roll
(For a 2 kg roll)

Ingredients
3 kg soft flour
1 kg sugar
½ water glass cinnamon for boiling
pounded mastic
3 tsp. salt
4 yeast sachets (dry yeast)
or ½ water glass fresh yeast

Preparation
Dissolve the fresh yeast in lukewarm water.
Put the flour in a bowl and add the dry
yeast or the dissolved yeast. Add the sugar,
salt and mastic, knead and add enough
water to make your dough soft.
Make a ring-shaped big roll and let it rise.
Add the ornaments (flowers made of
dough) on it and where there is space make
small holes using a toothpick. If you see that
the roll rises irregularly during baking, use
the toothpick to make small holes on it to
allow the air to evaporate.
Bake in the oven at 180° C. Test the bread
by pricking with a knife if it comes out dry,
the roll is ready.

Currant bread - Stafidopsomo

Ingredients
1 1/4 kg all purpose flour
650 gr. wheaten flour
3 tbsp. butter
1 tbsp. honey
3 tbsp. sugar
½ water glass milk or enough to knead
the dough
1 kg currants
mastic flavour

Preparation
Prepare the leaven by combining the
fresh yeast and lukewarm milk. The
next day, knead it and allow it to rise.
Then knead the mixture again, add the
currants and the mastic flavour and
make small buns. When they rise, bake
them in the oven at 200° C.

Dacos
(serves 4)

Ingredients
4 barley rusks (preferably round)
4 ripe tomatoes
salt
oil
oregano (optional)
1/4 kg fresh mizithra

Preparation
Slightly sprinkle the rusks with water.
Pour a tablespoon of oil on each rusk, or
more if preferred. Grate the fresh tomatoes and spread them over the rusks.
Season with salt and oregano finish with
fresh mizithra and your daco is ready.

Kalitsounia

It is a small pie (for 1 person), it is usually filled with mizithra but the filling can vary for example Malaka cheese (called Tiromalama) or filled with many kinds of local leafy greens, etc. Their shape can be either round (the Easter Kalitsounia in particular), semi-circular or square. They can be either baked or fried. They are consumed either as an appetiser - the savory cheese fillings and those filled with leafy greens - or as a dessert- the sweet cheese fillings. It is not known when they first appeared. They first started as a characteristic Easter dessert but nowadays they are consumed during the whole year. In the past, they were only prepared in houses, but nowadays several handicraft units make kalitsounakia of high quality and great variety, supplying hotels, restaurants, bakeries, chain-supermarkets and houses in both Crete and Athens.

Dough for Kalitsounia and pies
(20-30 Kalitsounia or one pie)

Ingredients
½ kg all purpose flour
½ tsp. salt
2 tbsp. oil
water (enough so that the dough does not stick in your hands when kneading it)
½ water glass tsikoudia

Preparation
Mix all the ingredients well, knead the dough with your hands and let it rise for 1-2 hours.

Preparation of pastry for Kalitsounia and pies

Kalitsounia:
Roll out the pastry using a rolling pin. Make a big pastry sheet, less than ½ cm thick and cut it in the shape of a tea saucer.

Pies:
Divide the dough and roll out 2 pastry sheets, one for the base and the other for the top.

Pies from Sfakia (Sfakianes pites)
(20-30 pieces)

Ingredients
½ kg mizithra
dough (see previous recipe)

Preparation
Take a small piece of dough (the size of an apricot), make it round, open it slightly in the middle, fill it with a tbsp. mizithra and close it again. Then slightly knead the dough and mizithra with your fingers, from the centre outwards, giving the pie the shape of a fruit plate. Then put it in a very hot non-stick frying pan and cook it without oil until it browns on both sides. It is served with honey on top.
Attention: Your success completely depends on how you roll out the pastry sheet, meaning that the sheet has to be very thin (2-3 millimetres).

Kalitsounia with spinach, fennel or wild local leafy greens (20-30 pieces)

Ingredients

1-1 ½ kg spinach or the other leafy greens
water glass, olive oil
salt, pepper, mint, sesame
1 onion, finely chopped

Preparation

For the preparation of the dough and pastry sheet see previous recipe. Remove the roots from the spinach, wash it well and cut it in small pieces. Saute it in an empty saucepan for 5 minutes, squeeze it with your hands and put it in a bowl. Add the onion, salt, pepper, mint, and oil and mix them. Using a rolling pin, roll out a pastry sheet the size of a small plate. Fill each pastry sheet with a tbsp. of the mixture and fold it closing its' ends well. Fry the Kalitsounia in sizzling oil on both sides or bake them in the oven for 20 minutes, at 180° C. If you are to bake the Kalitsounia, beat an egg yolk and glaze them, then sprinkle with sesame before baking.

Kalitsounia with mizithra, anthotiro or malaka (20 - 30 pieces)

Ingredients

1 kg mizithra or anthotiro or malaka
1 egg
1 tbsp. flour
1/2 water glass, olive oil
salt (optional)
For the preparation of the dough and
pastry sheet see the previous recipe.

Preparation

Put all the ingredients in a bowl and
mix them well. Put a tbsp. of the mixture on each pastry sheet, fold it, close
its' ends well and fry in sizzling oil on
both sides. Instead of using a frying
pan, you can bake the Kalitsounia in
the oven at 180° C, for about 20 minutes. In that case, beat an egg yolk and
glaze the Kalitsounia before putting
them in the oven.
Fried Kalitsounia are served with
honey or sprinkled with sugar.

Kalitsounia with aubergines
(20 - 30 pieces)

Ingredients

6-7 medium sized aubergines
2 large onions
½ water glass grated cheese
1/3 water glass, olive oil
2 eggs
salt

Easter Kalitsounia
(20 - 30 pieces)

Ingredients

1/4 kg anthotiro
1/4 kg mizithra
1/4 kg malaka
1 egg
mint (optional)
salt (optional)
sesame
1 tbsp. flour

Preparation

For the preparation of the dough and pastry sheet see the previous recipe. Combine all the ingredients in a bowl until uniform in texture. Put one tbsp. of the mixture in the centre of each pastry sheet and fold it in four, leaving it slightly open in the centre, right above the filling. Glaze the Kalitsounia with the egg yolk (using a small brush), sprinkle with plenty of sesame and put them in the oven at 180° C, for about 20 minutes.

Preparation

The night before, boil the aubergines and onions in plain water until they melt. Strain and leave them until the next morning. In a bowl combine the mashed aubergines, onions, salt, oil, cheese and eggs till uniform in texture. Roll out a pastry sheet (see: Dough and pastry sheet for Kalitsounia), prepare the Kalitsounia and either fry them in oil on both sides or put them in the oven (glaze with an egg yolk), at 180° C for 20 minutes.

Kalitsounia

Kalitsounia with wild celery, mint, salt and onion (20 - 30 pieces)

Ingredients
1 kg wild celery
1 tsp. mint
1 onion, finely chopped
salt

Preparation
Wash the wild celery well and chop it finely. Add the onion, mint and salt and make a smooth mixture.
Prepare the Kalitsounia as in the previous recipes and fry them in sizzling olive oil until golden brown on both sides.

Kalitsounia with onion, mizithra and basil (20 - 30 pieces)

Ingredients
4 - 5 large onions
1/4 kg mizithra
1 tsp. fresh basil
salt

Preparation
Slice the onions thinly add salt and fry them for 3 minutes. After the onions have cooled down, add the rest of the ingredients, make a smooth mixture, prepare the Kalitsounia as in the previous recipes and fry them in sizzling oil until they brown on both sides.

Kalitsounia with courgettes and mizithra (20 - 30 pieces)

Ingredients
4 -5 medium-sized courgettes or a big courgette
1/4 kg mizithra
1 onion, finely chopped
salt
1 tsp. fresh mint
1 egg

Preparation
Grate the courgettes, strain them and add the onion, mizithra, mint and salt. Make a smooth mixture and then roll out a pastry sheet (see previous recipes). Prepare the Kalitsounia, glaze with egg yolk and put them in the oven for 20 minutes, at 180° C.

41

Pies

Fennel pie (Marathopita)
(Medium sized baking pan, No 36)

Ingredients

1 kg fennel
1/2 water glass, olive oil
1 large onion, finely chopped
2 garlic cloves, finely chopped
1 tsp. salt
pepper
1 egg (if baking the pie)
1 tbsp. olive oil (for frying)

Preparation

Wash the fennel and chop it finely. Put it in a bowl, add the onion, garlic and salt and rub the ingredients well with your hands in order to strain the water. Then add the oil and pepper and mix them. Roll out a pastry sheet, the size of the baking pan, pour the mixture on it, spread it and cover with another pastry sheet of the same size, closing its' ends well in order for the filling not to spill.
Glaze the pie with an egg yolk and put it in the oven at 200°C, for ½ hour
If preferred, you can put the pie in a non-stick frying pan (where you will add 1 tbsp. oil) and fry lightly until golden brown on both sides.

Cheese pie
(Tiropita)
(Medium-sized baking pan, No 36)

Ingredients

½ kg feta cheese
2 eggs
some mint or dill or parsley
1 egg yolk
50 gr. sesame
dough (see previous recipes)

Preparation

Grate the feta in a large bowl, add the eggs and mint and mix them. Line a large baking pan with oil, cover it with a pastry sheet and oil it again, using a small brush. Pour the mixture in the pan and spread it over the pastry sheet. Cover the mixture with another pastry sheet, close it at the ends with you hands and glaze with egg yolk. Sprinkle with sesame, carve the pie in portions and put it in the oven for 40 minutes, at 200° C.

Spinach pie (Spanakopita)
(Medium-sized baking pan, No 36)

Ingredients
1 kg spinach
1 small onion, finely chopped
1 tsp. mint
½ tsp. salt
½ tsp. pepper
1/3 water glass, olive oil
1 egg yolk
50 gr. sesame

Preparation
Put the spinach in an empty
saucepan, saute it and then squeeze it
so as to remove the water. Add the
rest of the ingredients and mix them
to prepare the filling.
The rest of the procedure is the same
as in the recipe for the cheese pie.

Cream-filled pastry (Bougatsa)
(Medium-sized baking pan, No 36)

Ingredients
500 gr. mizithra
100 gr. staka
7 - 8 tbsp. all purpose flour
7 - 8 tbsp. butter
2 water glasses milk
½ kg phyllo puff pastry sheets (the
thinnest you can find, for baklava)

Preparation
Put the mizithra, staka and milk in a bowl
and whisk until the ingredients become a
fluffy soft cream. Using a small brush, line
a large baking pan with oil and put 4 pastry sheets in it one over the other, glazing
each sheet with oil separately. Spread the
mixture on the pastry sheets and fold
them in the shape of a parallelogram. Lay
4 pastry sheets on top, oiling each one of
them, and then invert the pie and fold the
pastry sheets again, giving them the shape
of a parallelogram. Bake the pie in the
oven (200° C) for 30 minutes. When serving the pie, you can sprinkle your piece
with sugar.

Cretan cannelloni with minced meat
(serves 8)

Ingredients

For the dough:
½ kg coarse flour
4 eggs
some salt

For the filling:

2 fresh onions, finely chopped
3/4 kg minced meat
½ water glass, olive oil
salt, pepper
1 tsp. cinnamon
2 tsp. oregano
1/2 water glass parsley
2 water glasses veal broth

To serve:

Dry anthotiros, grated (dry mizithra)

Preparation

Put the flour and some salt in a bowl and make a small hole in the middle. Beat the eggs and add them in the flour. Mix slowly with your hands until the dough becomes smooth. If the dough is sticky, add some flour and continue kneading for 5 more minutes. Leave the dough until it becomes firm. Saute the onions and minced meat in 3 tbsp. oil and add the salt, pepper, cinnamon, oregano and parsley. Add 1/4 water glass broth to the mixture and let it simmer for 10 minutes. Cut the dough in 4 pieces and roll out 4 thin pastry sheets. Cut the pastry sheets in squares (5 x 5 cm.). Put 2 tbsp. of filling in the middle of each pastry sheet. Make the cannelloni (rolls). Put them in a large oiled baking pan and glaze them with oil using a small brush. Bake the cannelloni in a pre-heated 150° C oven, for 25 minutes until they brown slightly. Pour the rest of the salted broth over them and continue baking for 20-25 minutes, at 180° C. Serve the cannelloni hot, together with the broth and grated cheese

Courgette and Potato Pie
(Chaniotiko Boureki)

Ingredients for the pastry sheet:
½ kg all purpose flour
3 tbsp. olive oil
½ tsp. salt
½ water glass red wine
about 1 glass of lukewarm water

For the filling:
1 ½ kg potatoes, cut in thin slices
1 ½ kg courgettes, cut in thin slices
a small bunch of mint
1 water glass all purpose flour
1 kg mizithra
200 gr. grated kasseri (kind of soft cheese)
about ½ water glass, olive oil
1 water glass milk
2 eggs
4 tbsp. staka
sesame, for sprinkling
salt, pepper

Preparation
Prepare the pastry sheet: put the water, oil, salt and wine in the flour and knead well. Cover the dough and leave it for about 30 minutes. Divide the dough in two and roll out two medium-sized pastry sheets. Lay one of them in a large baking pan lined with olive oil. Then add the potatoes, courgettes and mizithra in layers. Add some salt, pepper, mint, flour and kasseri over each layer. Beat the eggs with the milk and staka and pour the mixture over the patty. Then sprinkle with the oil, put the other pastry sheet on top, glaze with some oil and sprinkle with sesame. Cut the patty in square pieces and put it in the oven, which you have pre-heated at normal heat, for 20-25min, at 180° C.

Mizithra and Spinach Pie
(serves 6)

Ingredients
1 ½ kg spinach
800 gr. mizithra
½ water glass, olive oil
1 onion, finely chopped
salt, pepper
some milk or 1 egg
enough pastry sheet for a medium-sized baking pan, No 36

Preparation
Wash the spinach well and cut it to pieces. Saute it in a saucepan without water (10 minutes) and dry it off its' water, by rubbing it with your hands. Put the spinach, mizithra, oil, onion, salt and pepper in a bowl and mix them. Roll out a pastry sheet (see previous recipes), oil it, put it in the baking pan, add the mixture, cover with another pastry sheet and roll the 2 pastry sheets together on the inside. Glaze with egg or milk and put the patty in the oven, at 180° C, for about one hour.

Sweet Pumpkin Pie
(serves 4)

Ingredients
1 ½ kg pumpkin
1/4 kg mizithra
1/3 water glass, olive oil
2 tbsp. all purpose flour
salt, pepper

Preparation
Take the skin off the pumpkin, cut it in thin slices, add salt and pepper and sprinkle with the flour. Put a layer of pumpkin slices in a baking pan and add mizithra on top (spread it with your fingers). Make three layers (the last one being always mizithra), sprinkling each layer with oil, and bake the patty in the oven at 180°C, for 1 ½ hour.

Pumpkin Pie (Kolokithopita)
(Medium-sized baking pan, No 36)

Ingredients for the filling:
1 ½ kg grated courgettes
1 kg mizithra
5-6 mint leaves

For the bechamel sauce:
3 tbsp. soft flour
4 tbsp. olive oil
2 water glasses lukewarm milk
a pinch of salt
3 eggs

For the crust:
½ water glass milk
4 tbsp. crushed rusk
2 tbsp. coarse flour
3 tbsp. olive oil
2 eggs
small portion of butter

For the pastry sheet:
½ kg coarse flour
½ water glass, olive oil
a pinch of salt

Preparation
Wash the courgettes well, grate and boil them in water for 10 minutes. Let them strain for 2 hours.

For the bechamel sauce:
Put the oil in a saucepan. When it starts to sizzle, add the flour and mix gently for 2 minutes. Add the lukewarm milk slowly until the mixture becomes a cream, neither thick nor thin, and then add the salt. Remove from the fire, add the eggs, mix well, add the mizithra, mint and courgettes and mix well once more.

For the pastry sheet:
Put the flour in an enamel bowl, make a small hole in the middle and add the oil and salt. Knead them, adding water bit by bit, until you prepare a soft pliable dough. Then roll out the pastry sheet using a rolling-pin. Line a baking pan with oil and put the pastry sheet inside, so that it covers the whole baking pan and its' sides. Then pour the filling over the pastry sheet and lay the crust on top.

For the crust:
Beat the eggs in a small bowl. Add the rusks, flour, milk, butter and oil. Beat the mixture until it becomes smooth and pour it in the baking pan, after having added the last pastry sheet. Put the pie in the oven, which you have pre-heated at normal heat, and bake for about 1 hour at 200° C. When the pie is almost done, place a grease-proof paper over the baking pan.

Greens & Salads

Sprouts with fresh broad beans
(serves 4)

Ingredients
1 kg sprouts
½ kg fresh broad beans
1 lemon
olive oil, salt

Preparation
Wash the greens and broad beans well (if the broad beans are very tender leave them unshelled) and boil them in hot water for 40 minutes. Then strain them, put them in a large flat dish and add the lemon juice, olive oil and salt.
και το αλάτι.

Fried ascrolibri

Ingredients
1 kg ascrolibri
olive oil, flour, salt

Preparation
Wash the ascrolibri well, clean them, keeping only their roots and throw away the rest. Sprinkle with salt and flour and fry them in the oil until they are golden brown on both sides.

Ascrolibri with broad beans
(serves 4)

Ingredients
½ kg ascrolibri
½ lemon
olive oil, salt
½ kg dried broad beans (optional)

Preparation
Wash the ascrolibri, wash them well and boil them in hot water for ½ hour. Then strain them, put them in a large flat dish and add the oil, lemon juice and salt.
If you want, you can add ½ kg dried broad beans, which you boil with the greens, after having soaked them in water for one night.

Mashed broad beans (Koukia trifta or thrifta)

Ingredients

½ kg dried broad beans
olive oil, vinegar, mint,
oregano, salt

Preparation

The day before, put the broad beans in water and let them soak
during the whole night. The next day, rinse them, put them in a
saucepan with plenty of water and boil them at low heat for 1 to
1 ½ hour (until they become very soft).
Then strain, salt and put them in the blender (together with
their hull). Season with some oil, vinegar, mint and oregano,
mix and serve.

Notchweeds & Stifnos (serves 4)

Notchweeds saute

(serves 6)

Ingredients

1 ½ kg notchweeds
½ kg stifnos
2-3 courgettes
200 gr. string beans
2/3 water glass, olive oil
3-4 garlic cloves
2 ripe tomatoes, grated
1/2 water glass red wine
salt, pepper

Preparation

Clean and wash the greens and string beans well. Cut the courgettes in half. Put the oil in a casserole and when it starts to sizzle, add the greens, string beans and courgettes. Boil them for 4-5 minutes and add the wine. Add the garlic, salt, pepper and some water (if needed) and cook the food for 15-20 minutes.
(If you want, you can also add the tomatoes together with the water).

Ingredients

1 kg notchweeds and stifnos
1 lemon
1 big tomato
olive oil, salt
2-3 potatoes (optional)
2-3 courgettes (optional)

Preparation

Wash the greens well and boil them in very hot water for ½ hour, together with the tomato cut in half. Then strain them, put them in a large flat dish and add the oil, lemon juice and salt.
If you want, you can add 2-3 potatoes cut in big pieces and 2-3 courgettes cut in half, which you boil together with the greens.

Greens saute or sprouts casserole
(serves 6)

Ingredients

1 kg various local greens *, not the
ones we usually boil
1 large onion, finely chopped
½ kg spinach
4 garlic cloves
½ water glass, olive oil
½ kg ripe tomatoes, grated
salt, pepper
2-3 potatoes
4-5 courgettes

Preparation

Clean the greens and wash them
well. Put the oil in a saucepan and
brown the onion and garlic. Add
the greens and spinach bit by bit and
cook until they soften. Then add the
tomatoes, salt and pepper and cook
for 20 minutes at normal heat.
If you want, you can add potatoes
cut in thick slices and courgettes cut
in two, which you put in the casserole just before adding the tomatoes.
* Lagoudohorto, koutsounares, wild
parsley.

Chicory or Stamnagkathi
(serves 4)

Ingredients

1 kg chicory or stamnagkathi
1 lemon
olive oil, salt

Preparation

Clean the greens, wash them well and
boil them in very hot water for ½ hour.
Then strain them, put them in a large
flat dish and add the oil, lemon and salt.
The chicory and stamnagkathi can also
be eaten raw, without oil. Clean and
wash them and add the lemon and salt.

Pickled bulbs (serves 4)

Salad with avronies

Ingredients
1 kg avronies
salt
olive oil
lemon

Preparation
Clean the avronies, wash them well and cut them in pieces. Boil them for 10-12 minutes. Strain them (keep their stock), put them in a large flat dish and add salt, some oil and lemon. A fine salad with a special, bitter taste. One can drink the stock since it has various healing properties.

Ingredients
1 ½ kg bulbs
½ water glass, olive oil
vinegar, salt

Preparation
Wash the bulbs well and remove their shell, as you do with the onions. Boil them in salted water for 20-30 minutes and then soak them in clean water for 2-3 days. Change the water 2- 3 times per day until their bitterness is washed away (if you like them slightly bitter, leave them in the water less and salt them fewer times). Then rinse them, put them in a vase filled with vinegar and add ½ water glass oil in order for the air not to pass through easily.

Fried agoglossi (wild nettle)

Ingredients

½ kg agoglossi
1 water glass, olive oil
1 water glass flour
salt

Preparation

Use only the tender part (heart) of the greens. Wash them well and scald them. Prepare the batter (mix the flour and water in a bowl until the mixture becomes mushy). Salt the greens, dip them in the batter and fry them in sizzling oil.

Salad with rusk, artichoke & mizithra

Ingredients

1 barley rusk, cut in small pieces
2-3 artichokes
3 tbsp. mizithra
salt, pepper, oregano
2 medium-sized tomatoes
1 small onion, preferably fresh
olive oil
A handful of olives from Selinos (seliniotikes)

Preparation

Put the rusk at the bottom of a salad bowl. Chop all the ingredients and lay them on the rusk (last of all the mizithra). Sprinkle with oregano and add the olive oil and olives

Salad with boiled wild asparagus (serves 4)

Ingredients

1 kg wild asparagus
salt, olive oil, lemon juice

Preparation

Clean the asparagus, wash them well and cut them. Boil them for 10-12 minutes. Strain them (keep the stock), put them in a large flat dish and add salt, oil and lemon. Keep the stock and drink it since it has various healing properties.

Spinach puree

Ingredients

1 kg spinach
2 tbsp. fresh butter
some flour (all purpose)
nutmeg
pounded clove
salt
1 water glass milk

Preparation

Boil the spinach in water. When it is done, strain it and then cool it with some cold water. Strain it again and use it to make small balls, which you will break up with a small knife. Put the butter and flour in a small casserole, bring the mixture to the boil and add the spinach, which you have squeezed well. Stir the food and add the salt and flavourings. Cook the spinach for 10 minutes and then add the milk and mix until the food candies.

Fish-roe salad (serves 4)

Ingredients

100gr white fish-roe
3 slices stale bread
1 cup olive oil
1 small onion, finely chopped
Juice of 1 ½ lemons

Preparation

Soak bread in a bowl of water for 2-3 minutes. Remove the breadcrumb and squeeze to drain excess water. In another bowl place the fish roe and breadcrumb and stir continuously. Then, stir in the oil and the lemon gradually. Bear in mind that the mixture should be beaten very well. You can use a blender to produce a uniform mixture, but make sure that it does not become too creamy. Garnish with finely chopped onion.

Country style salad (Horiatiki) (serves 4)

Ingredients

2 large tomatoes
2 cucumbers
Some feta or mizithra cheese
2-3 small rusks
2-3 small, fresh peppers
Olives
1 small cup olive oil
Salt - oregano

Preparation

In a large bowl cut the tomatoes and the cucumbers into slices, crumble the rusks and chop the peppers. Season with salt, pour the oil and mix well. Top with the cheese, the olives and sprinkle with oregano.

Lima beans salad
(serves 6)

Ingredients

½ kilo lima beans
1 medium onion
3-4 tablespoons oil
A little lemon juice
2-3 teaspoons parsley, finely chopped
Salt

Preparation

Soak the beans overnight in water to soften. Boil them for about 35-40 minutes in plenty of water and afterwards strain and place them in another bowl. Add salt, chopped onion, parsley, oil and mix well

Tzatziki
(serves 4)

Ingredients

½ kilo strained yoghurt
2-3 tablespoons oil
Very little vinegar
2 large cucumbers, grated
5-6 cloves of garlic, mashed
Some dill, finely chopped
Salt - white pepper

Preparation

Squeeze the cucumbers very well to drain water. Place all ingredients in a bowl and mix well, until you get a uniform mixture. At the end, sprinkle with the finely chopped dill.

* Tzatziki: A cold appetising dip made with yogurt, cucumber, olive oil and garlic

Aubergine salad
(serves 4)

Ingredients

½ kilo large aubergines
1 cup olive oil
1 lemon, juiced
2-3 cloves of garlic, finely chopped
Some feta cheese, finely chopped
(optional)
Salt - pepper

Preparation

Prick the aubergines with a fork and bake them in the oven at low temperature until their peel is charred. Then skin them carefully and place them in a bowl. Add salt, pepper, lemon juice and mix well for some time. Combine with the finely chopped garlic, slowly pour in the oil in small quantities and keep on stirring until the mixture becomes uniform. At the end, you can optionally sprinkle with finely chopped feta cheese.

Artichokes

Boiled artichokes
(serves 4)

Ingredients
6 medium-sized artichokes
3 medium-sized potatoes
4 small courgettes
½ water glass, olive oil
salt, pepper
lemon juice

Preparation
Clean, wash and cut the artichokes in
four. Put them in a bowl filled with
water and some lemon juice in
order for them not to turn black.
Cut the potatoes and courgettes in
thick slices, put them in a saucepan,
cover with water, add salt and pepper and boil the food for 10 minutes. Then add the oil and continue
boiling for 10-15 minutes at normal heat.
When serving the artichokes, you can add
some lemon juice in your plate.

Raw artichokes
with lemon
(serves 4)

Ingredients
4-5 big artichokes
the juice of 2 lemons
½ handful of flour (for all uses)
salt

Preparation
Clean the artichokes and
cut them in four. Put
each artichoke you
clean in a small bowl
filed with water and
flour. This way the
artichokes will not
blacken. After cleaning
them, take them out
of the bowl and wash
them. Finally, rub each
artichoke with lemon, cut them
in smaller pieces and serve in a soup
plate, adding lemon and salt.

Artichokes with minced meat or artichokes moussaka (serves 6)

Ingredients

6 big artichokes
½ kg minced meat
½ water glass, olive oil
1 large onion, finely chopped
salt, pepper

Preparation

Clean, wash and cut the artichokes in pieces. In the mean while, brown the minced meat for 15 minutes, having added the onion, salt and pepper. Put a layer of artichokes in a baking pan, then a layer of minced meat and again a layer of artichokes. Pour some oil over the food and put it in the oven for 1 hour, at 180° C. If you want, you can pour bechamel sauce over the food.

Artichokes with broad beans, potatoes, tomatoes (serves 6)

Ingredients

6 medium-sized artichokes
1 kg fresh broad beans
3 medium-sized potatoes, cut in four
3 medium-sized ripe tomatoes, grated
1 water glass, olive oil
1 large onion, finely chopped
salt, pepper

Preparation

Clean, wash and cut the artichokes in four. Put them in a bowl filled with water and some lemon juice in order for them not to turn black. Clean the broad beans and keep their inside and some pods, if they are very tender. Put the oil in a saucepan and when it starts to sizzle, add the onion and broad beans and brown them for 5-7 minutes. Add the artichokes, cook for 3-5 minutes and then add the tomatoes, salt and pepper and continue cooking for 10 minutes. Finally, add the potatoes and some water, if needed, and simmer at low heat, for 15-20 minutes.

Artichokes with broad beans
(serves 6)

Ingredients
6 medium-sized artichokes
1 kg broad beans
1 water glass, olive oil
2 tbsp. dill, finely chopped
the juice of 2 medium-sized lemons
1 tbsp. flour (for all uses)
salt, pepper

Preparation
Clean and wash the artichokes and broad beans (see previous recipe). Put the oil in a saucepan and when it starts to sizzle, add the broad beans and dill and cook for 5-7 minutes. Then add the artichokes, some water, salt and pepper and cook for 20-25 minutes at normal heat. Put the lemon juice and flour in a big glass and mix them very well in order for the flour to dissolve completely. Three minutes before removing the food from the fire, add the mixture in the saucepan and stir the food well.

Artichokes filled with baked staka
(serves 4)

Ingredients
The heads of 8 artichokes
50 gr. butter made from staka, melted
8 tbsp. baked staka
salt

Preparation
Clean the artichokes, leave some tender leaves in their heart and, using a knife, remove the inside of each artichoke carefully, making some space. Boil the artichokes for 15 minutes, salt them and then put a tbsp. baked staka in each one of them. Lay them in a baking pan, sprinkle with the butter, and put them in the oven (180 -200° C) for about 1 hour, until golden brown.

Artichokes with rusk
(serves 6)

Ingredients
6-8 big artichokes
juice of 1 lemon
2 eggs
2 rusks, crushed
1/2 water glass grated cheese
2/3 water glass, olive oil
salt, pepper
lemon peel, cut in slices

Preparation
Clean the artichokes and cut them in half. Boil them for 15 minutes in water, where you have added the salt, lemon juice and lemon peel. Throw away the water and add salt and pepper. Beat the eggs in a bowl and put the rusks and cheese in another bowl. Dip the artichokes first in the eggs and then in the rusks, and fry them in sizzling oil until golden brown on both sides.
Serve them with eggs sfougato.

Dishes cooked in olive oil & Various Dishes

Stuffed vegetables in the oven or in the saucepan
(serves 6-8)

Ingredients

5 medium-sized ripe tomatoes
4 medium-sized peppers
5 medium-sized courgettes
4 long and narrow-shaped aubergines
½ water glass, water + ½ water glass, olive oil
2 large onions, finely chopped
2 tbsp. parsley, mint
1 tbsp. fennel
½ kg rice (simple)
10 vine leaves
salt, pepper

Preparation

Wash the vegetables well and take out their insides. Grate the inside of the tomatoes and courgettes, put it in a bowl, add ½ water glass oil, the onions, flavourings, rice, salt and pepper and mix them. Put the vegetables in a large baking pan and stuff them with the mixture. Add 1 ½ glass of water and ½ water glass oil, cover the food with the vine leaves in order for its' surface not to dry and bake at 200° C for 1 ½ hour, in a pre-heated oven.

For the saucepan:

Put all the ingredients in a large saucepan, cover them with water, cover the saucepan with a soup plate and boil the food at normal heat for 40 minutes.

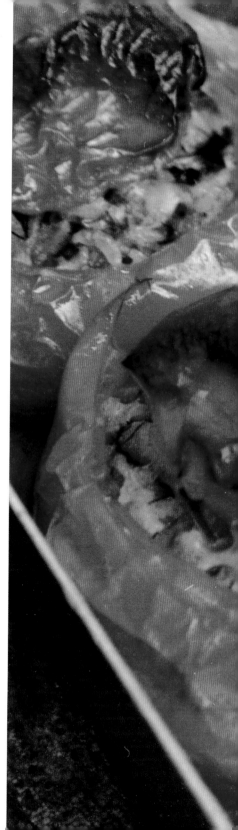

Dolmadakia with vine leafs or sorrels or pumpkin tops and flowers (in the saucepan or in the oven)
(serves 8)

Ingredients

½ water glass, olive oil
½ kg rice used for stuffing vegetables
salt, pepper, oregano
1 tsp. parsley, mint
1 ripe tomato, grated
4 small onions, finely chopped
½ lemon
40 vine leaves or sorrels or
pumpkin tops and flowers
2 medium-sized potatoes, cut
in slices

Preparation

Scald the vine leaves (put water in a saucepan and when it comes to the boil, put them inside and leave them for 2 minutes, turning them on both sides). If you are to use sorrels, you have to be very careful. Dip them into boiling water until they soften on both sides. You don't need to scald the pumpkin tops and flowers.

For the filling:

Put the oil, onions, rice, flavourings, salt, pepper and tomato (optional) in a bowl. Mix them well and fill the pumpkin tops and flowers, sorrels or vine leaves with the mixture, using a tsp. Fold them and put them in a large saucepan, after having covered its' bottom with potato slices in order for the food not to stick. Add some water, enough to cover the dolmadakia, cover them with a plate, boil at high heat and when they come to the boil, lower the heat and cook for ½ hour. Add the lemon in the rice or in the water in order for the rice not to mash. If you want, you can use meat broth instead of water (of course the food is much tastier this way). If you are to cook the dolmadakia in the oven, put them in a large baking pan and cover them with water (not completely) and vine leaves or sorrels. Bake the food for about one hour, at 200° C.

Meatballs with anthotiro

Ingredients

½ kg anthotiro
2 eggs
1 tbsp. flour
½ water glass, olive oil

Preparation

Put the anthotiro and flour in a bowl and knead
them until the mixture becomes smooth. Then
use the mixture to make small balls. Beat the
eggs in a bowl, dip the balls in it one by one and
fry them in sizzling oil until they are golden
brown.

Casserole from Selino (Stifado)
(serves 4)

Ingredients

½ water glass, olive oil
½ kg small onions (for stew)
2 ripe tomatoes, grated
1/4 kg sour hondro
½ water glass red wine
salt, pepper, 2 bay leaves
8 - 10 boiled chestnuts, peeled and cut in 4

Preparation

Brown the onions in the oil. Add salt, pepper and the wine. Cook for 2 minutes and then add the tomatoes. Continue cooking for 15 minutes until the food is almost ready and then add the hondro. Add the bay leaves and some water, if needed. Five minutes before removing the casserole from the fire, add the chestnuts, mix well and bring to the boil in order for the food to thicken.

Lentil-rice
(serves 4)

Preparation

Cook the lentils as usual, adding some extra water. Add 4 tbsp. rice used for soups and boil for 10 minutes. This soup becomes a little thicker than lentil-soup.

Chickpeas with bitter oranges (serves 4)

Ingredients
½ kg chickpeas
1/4 water glass, olive oil
2 medium-sized bitter oranges
5 tbsp. flour
2 medium-sized onions, finely chopped
salt, pepper

Preparation
The previous nigh soak the chickpeas in water. In the morning, put them in a saucepan half-full with water and start boiling them. Skim them and when they are soft enough, add the onions and oil. In the mean while, squeeze the bitter oranges and add the flour, salt and pepper in their juice, mixing very well so that the flour dissolves completely. When the chickpeas are ready *, add the mixture in the saucepan and cook at low heat until the soup becomes thick (about 5 minutes).
*The time you will need to boil the chickpeas, depends on their quality and variety. It usually ranges from 1 to 2 hours.
Note: The chickpeas have to be unshelled.

Chickpea-rice (serves 4)

Preparation
When the chickpeas have been cooked and after having added the bitter oranges' mixture in the saucepan, strain them, put them in a large flat dish and keep their stock. Add 1½ water glass of rice in the stock and cook the food long enough for the rice to remain granular. Leave the rice cool for a while, add it in the chickpeas, mix well and gently and garnish with fresh parsley. The ideal solution when you have some chickpeas left over, is to prepare a summer salad, adding fresh tomato, cucumber, feta, parsley and purslane.

Macaroni Skioufikta

Ingredients

1/2 kg flour
1 glass of water
1 tsp. salt
3 tbsp. Cretan olive oil
1 cup grated anthotiros cheese
1-2 tbsp. butter

Preparation

Knead the flour with the water, the salt and the olive oi. Leave the dough for one hour and then make the macaroni. Mould the dough into finger-sized strips and cut it in small pieces (about 3cm long). Then put a finger in the middle of each piece and form a short and fat macaroni, which is empty in the middle. Spread some flour on the table, place the macaroni on it and let them dry for about an hour. Then shift them and boil them for approximately half an hour. Serve them in a deep plate with a drilled dipper and them pour hot butter (preferably "staka butter") and sprinkle the grated anthotiros cheese on top.

Fried pumpkin

Ingredients

3/4 kg pumpkin
some flour
salt

Preparation

Wash, clean and cut the pumpkin in long and narrow pieces. Salt, flour and fry the pieces in sizzling oil on both sides.

Courgettes with cheese
(serves 4)

Ingredients

½ kg courgettes
½ water glass, olive oil
2 ripe tomatoes, grated
250 gr. dry anthotiro, grated
salt, pepper

Preparation

Wash and clean the courgettes and cut them in long and narrow pieces. Fry them in the oil and when they are done, add the tomatoes, some water, salt and pepper. Cook them for 10 minutes at low heat. Then sprinkle with the cheese and continue cooking for 12 minutes, so that the food stays oily.

Various Dishes

Aubergines "Papoutsakia"
(serves 4)

Ingredients

7-8 medium-sized aubergines
5-6 large onions, finely chopped
3/4 water glass, olive oil
5-6 mashed tomatoes or 5-6 fresh tomatoes, peeled
3-4 tbsp. crushed rusk
2-3 tbsp. finely chopped parsley
2 tbsp. grated cheese
3 eggs
salt, pepper

Preparation

The aubergines have to be of regular shape. Cut them in half, remove their insides bit by bit, chop it finely and keep it. Boil the aubergines for a few minutes in order to soften. Put them in a bowl in rows and salt them. Put the oil in a saucepan, brown the onions and then add the tomato, parsley, salt, pepper and the inside of the aubergines. Simmer until all the liquid evaporates. Then remove from the fire, beat the eggs, mix them well with the cheese and stuff the aubergines with the mixture. Line a baking pan with plenty of oil and put the aubergines inside, in rows. Then beat one egg, pour it over the food and finally sprinkle with some cheese and crushed rusk. Bake the food in the oven for about 1 ½ hour, at 180°C.

Aubergines with sour hondro (serves 6)

Ingredients

1 ½ kg long and narrow-shaped ripe
aubergines, cut in thick slices
½ water glass sour hondro
4 medium-sized ripe tomatoes, grated
2 medium-sized onions, finely chopped
6-7 garlic cloves
1 bay leaf
2-3 pimento grains
½ water glass, olive oil
salt
1 small paprika
1 water glass red wine
2-3 potatoes (optional)

Preparation

Dissolve the sour hondro in some lukewarm
water. Brown the onions, garlic, pimento,
bay leaf and paprika in the oil and add salt.
After they have softened (2-3 minutes), add
the wine and then the tomatoes and
aubergines. Cook for 15-20 minutes, add
the sour hondro in the casserole and continue cooking for 3-5 minutes. If preferred,
you can also add 2-3 medium-sized potatoes, cut in thick slices, after having added
the aubergines.

Aubergines souffle (with Rusk & Cheese)

Ingredients

½ kg aubergines
½ water glass rusk, crushed
A handful of grated cheese
½ water glass milk
2 eggs
2 tbsp. fresh butter
salt, pepper

Preparation

Take the aubergines, shell them and cut
them in small pieces. "Sweeten" them (leave
them for 5-10 minutes in a bowl filled with
water and some vinegar in order to soak the
bitterness out of them) and then scald them.
When they have boiled, throw their water,
mash them and add salt and pepper. Beat
the egg whites and yolks separately and then
mix all the ingredients together. Pour the
mixture in a large baking pan lined with butter and sprinkled with crushed rusk. Then
sprinkle with crushed rusk and a tbsp. butter
and put the food in the oven. Instead of
sprinkling the souffle with rusk, you can
pour bechamel sauce over it.

Pastitsio* (serves 8)

Ingredients

½ kilo bucatini or ziti pasta
½ kilo minced beef
1/2 cup olive oil
2-3 medium size, ripe tomatoes
1 small glass red wine
200gr yellow cheese, grated
1 onion, finely chopped
1 tablespoon fresh butter
Salt - pepper

Preparation

Saute the oil and the onion in a medium-sized saucepan until golden and stir in the minced beef. Stir for 3-4 minutes and extinguish with wine. Add the tomatoes, season with salt and pepper and cook for another 20-25 minutes. If necessary, pour in some more water. In a large pot add water and a tablespoon of salt. Bring to boil, add the macaroni and stir. Boil for about 15 minutes. Strain and mix with a tablespoon of butter. In a large baking pan spread the boiled macaroni, cover with minced-meat and sprinkle with some cheese. Use the rest of the cheese to prepare the bechamel sauce and then pour the sauce on top of the pastitsio to cover it completely. Bake at 180oC for 40-45 minutes until lightly brown.

* Pastitsio: Layered dish with ziti pasta, minced beef and cheese topped with bechamel sauce.

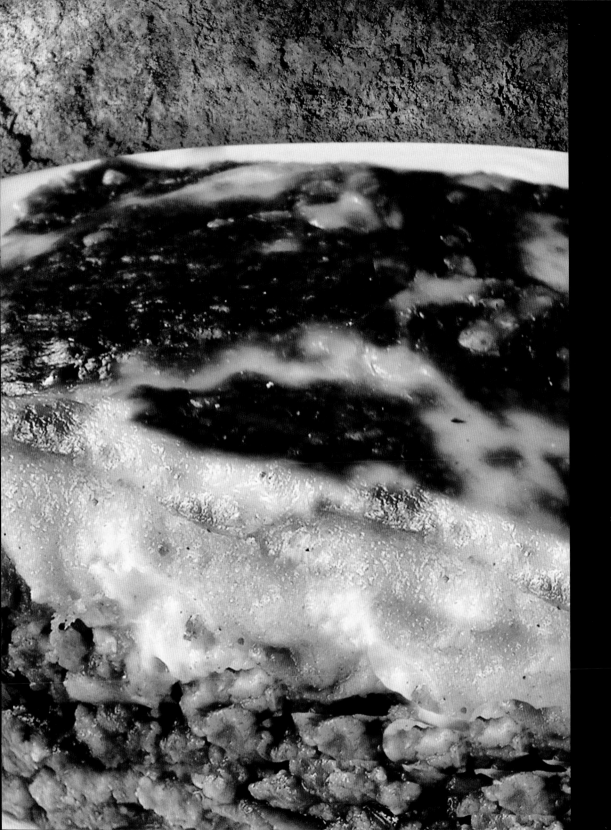

Moussakas
(serves 8)

Ingredients
1 kilo aubergines, cut into rounds
1 kilo potatoes, cut into rounds
2 cups olive oil
1/2 kilo minced beef
1 glass red wine
1 onion, finely chopped
2-3 ripe tomatoes, grated
200gr yellow cheese, grated
Salt - pepper

Preparation
Fry the aubergines and the potatoes and then drain for 2-3 hours to remove excess oil. Subsequently, cook the minced meat (see recipe for pastitsio). In a baking pan spread out a layer of potatoes, cover with aubergines and a then place a layer of minced meat. Keep on alternating the layers of potatoes, aubergines and minced meat until all ingredients are exhausted and top evenly with minced meat. Combine the bechamel sauce with cheese and pour on top. Bake in the oven at 180oC for 40-45 minutes, until the cream turns lightly brown.

Amanites or Manites (Mushrooms)

Amanites* with oregano and lemon, baked or grilled

Ingredients

1 ½ kg amanites
½ water glass, olive oil
½ water glass lemon juice
salt, pepper, oregano

Preparation

Clean the amanites and wash them well. Put them in a large baking pan together with the oil, lemon juice, salt, pepper and oregano. Grill them for 20-25 minutes. Following the same procedure, you can also barbecue the mushrooms. They are much tastier this way.

*Amanites or Manites are a kind of wild mushroom, with a big and flat surface, which is in profusion in Chania. Nowadays, you can also find amanites in the market.

Amanites casserole with chestnuts (Koumarites) (serves 4)

Ingredients4

1 ½ kg amanites
½ kg onions
½ water glass, olive oil
2 medium-sized ripe tomatoes
3/4 kg chestnuts
salt, pepper

Preparation

Follow the procedure described in the recipe "Amanites casserole". In the mean while, carve the chestnuts and either boil them or bake them in the oven (20 minutes). Peel them and add them in the casserole 10 minutes before the food is ready.

Amanites (Mushrooms)

Hadiarofouskes * (Slate-coloured mushrooms)

Ingredients

1 ½ kg hadiarofouskes
1 handful of flour (all purpose)
rosemary
olive oil
salt

Preparation

Clean the mushrooms, salt and slightly flour them and fry them in the oil for 5-7 minutes, adding some rosemary.
* Hadiarofouskes or Slate-coloured mushrooms: a kind of wild mushroom that is found at the foot of Lefka Ori (we ate it at the village named Karanou, which is just before Omalos). The mushroom grows in the ground. I would say that it is the "truffle" of the south-eastern Mediterranean.

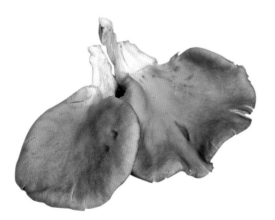

Amanites casserole (Stifado)

(serves 4)

Ingredients

1 ½ kg amanites
½ kg onions, cut in thick slices
½ water glass, olive oil
2 medium-sized ripe tomatoes, grated
salt, pepper

Preparation

Clean the amanites and wash them well. Put the oil in a frying pan and when it starts to sizzle, add the amanites, fry them for 2-3 minutes and then add the onions, salt and pepper. Five minutes later, add the tomatoes and cook the food at normal heat for 20-25 minutes.

Cabbage (frio*) casserole

(serves 6)

Ingredients

A piece of frio (about 1 kg)
3 medium-sized potatoes, cut in slices
½ kg onions, cut in thick slices
2 big ripe tomatoes, grated
3 garlic cloves
1 water glass, olive oil
salt, pepper

Preparation

Wash and cut the frio in pieces. Brown the onions and garlic in the oil. 2-3 minutes later add the potatoes and frio, stir 2-3 times, add the tomatoes, salt and pepper and cook the food at normal heat for 20-25 minutes.
* It is not a cabbage, it's just being called that. It is a kind of mushroom that grows on the roots and trunk of chestnut trees. Its' taste is very similar to that of chicken breast.

Mushroom soup

(serves 6)

Ingredients

1 kg mushrooms, finely chopped
1 medium sized onion
1 cup olive oil
½ cup spring onions, finely chopped
½ cup dill
½ small cup white wine
Salt - pepper
For the egg-lemon sauce
1 egg
1 lemon, juiced (see recipe for lamb with spiny chicory)

Preparation

Clean and rinse the mushrooms. In a pot saute the oil and the finely chopped onion until slightly brown and, then, add the mushrooms. Season with salt and pepper and let simmer for 2-3 minutes. Extinguish with wine, add 3-4 cups of water and let boil for 20-25 minutes. Then, add the spring onions and the dill and let everything simmer for 10-15 until thoroughly cooked. When done, remove from heat and pour in the egg-lemon sauce.

Fried amanites

Ingredients
1 ½ kg amanites
½ water glass, olive oil
½ water glass flour
salt, pepper

Preparation
Clean the amanites and wash
them well. Add salt and pepper,
flour them slightly and fry them
in sizzling oil for 5-10 minutes.
If you want you can also add
some vinegar before you take
them of the fire.

Snails

They are molluscs, they are either thin or thick and their colour
is either dark brown, light brown or whitish. Snails are always
picked in autumn when the first rains start. They are picked
from areas where there are vineyards, bushes and rocks. In these
areas, the snails eat fine self-sown herbs and that is why they are
extremely tasty. Put them inside a deep woven basket (so as not
to "escape"), always keep them in a dark and cool place and add
pasta or flour in the basket for about 5 days, in order for the
snails to be fed and "cleaned". Then take them out, clean them
and repeat the feeding procedure for 2-3 days.
The summer snails are called skalisti and you can cook them
right away, without having to feed them.

Preparation

Put the snails in a big bowl filled with water and leave them
there until their heads come out (30 to 45 minutes) and clean
them thoroughly. Throw away all the snails whose heads have
not come out. Put the snails in a saucepan half-full with water
and when the water comes to the boil, add a tbsp. salt and boil
them for 10 minutes. Then throw the water and wash them
very well with cold water.

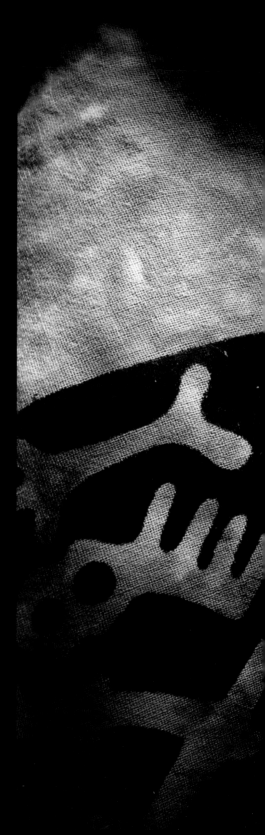

Snails with potatoes and courgettes
(serves 6)

Ingredients
1 kg snails
6 medium-sized potatoes, cut in slices
5 courgettes
3 medium-sized ripe tomatoes, grated
2/3 water glass, olive oil
1 medium-sized onion, cut in slices
3 garlic cloves
1/2 a bunch of parsley
salt, pepper

Preparation
Put the oil in a saucepan and when it starts to sizzle, add the snails, onion, garlic, parsley, salt and pepper and brown them for 2-3 minutes. Then add the potatoes, tomatoes and courgettes and continue cooking at low heat for about 20 minutes. If needed add some water.

Boiled snails
(serves 6)

Ingredients
1 kg snails
1 medium-sized ripe tomato cut in half
salt, oregano

Preparation
Put the snails in a saucepan, add enough water to cover them, add salt, some oregano and the tomato and boil at normal heat for 15-20 minutes.
Boiled snails are eaten dipped in sauce vinegraitte, mainly on Good Friday and Shrove Monday.
It is customary to pour some oil over the snails, when putting them on the plate.

Snails casserole (Stifado)
(serves 6)

Ingredients
1 kg snails
1 kg small onions (for stew)
3 medium-sized ripe tomatoes, grated
2/3 water glass, olive oil
salt, pepper

Preparation
Put the oil in a saucepan and when it starts to sizzle, add the snails, stir 2-3 times and after 4-5 minutes, add salt, pepper and the onions. After the food has come to the boil twice (about 5 minutes), add the tomatoes, lower the heat to normal and simmer for 30- 35 minutes.

Snails with pilaff
(serves 6)

Ingredients
1 kg snails
2/3 water glass, olive oil
2 medium-sized ripe tomatoes,
grated
1½ water glass, rice
salt, pepper

Preparation
Put the oil in a saucepan and
when it starts to sizzle, add the
snails and cook them for 2-3
minutes. Add salt, pepper and
the tomatoes and continue cooking for 15 minutes at normal
heat. Then add 4 ½ glasses of
water and when the food comes
to the boil, add the rice and continue cooking for about 15-20
minutes, stirring often in order
for the food not to stick.

Snails with rosemary and wine (boubouristi) (serves 6)

Ingredients

1 kg snails
½ water glass, red wine
½ water glass, flour (all purpose)
½ water glass, olive oil
salt, pepper, rosemary

Preparation

Salt the snails, flour them and cook them in sizzling oil for 3 minutes, with their openings facing the pan. Add the rosemary, salt and pepper, stir them and 2 minutes later add the wine. Bring them to the boil and they are ready to be served. Another option is to prepare a batter, using flour, salt, pepper, oregano and garlic (optional), fill the snails' openings with this mixture and fry them in the oil and rosemary.

Snails with hondro
(serves 6)

Ingredients
1 kg snails
2 ripe tomatoes, grated
1 large onion, finely chopped
1 ½ glass hondro (Ground wheat of very fine quality. You can find it in the market).
2/3 water glass, olive oil
salt, pepper

Preparation
Brown the onion in the oil. When it is ready, add the snails and cook for 2 minutes. Then add the tomatoes, salt and pepper, continue cooking for 10 minutes and add the water. When the food comes to the boil, add the hondro and cook for 15 minutes, stirring continuously in order for the food not to stick.
Use soup plates for serving this food and let saucepan it thicken slightly. It becomes an excellent cream. You can also eat it cold the following day.
The exact same preparation also goes for sour hondro.

Boiled snails (Lianides*) with garlic paste
(serves 6)

Ingredients
1 kg snails (lianides)
1 medium-sized ripe tomato, cut in four
salt, pepper
For the garlic paste:
5-6 garlic cloves
2 slices of bread (dry, soaked and strained of its' water)
1 water glass, olive oil
2 tbsp. vinegar
salt

Preparation
Put the snails in a saucepan, add enough water to cover them, add the salt, pepper and tomato and cook at normal heat for about 15-20 minutes.
After boiling the lianides (see recipe "Boiled snails"), prepare the garlic paste in a mortar and eat the lianides dipping them in the garlic paste.
*Lianides are the thin and small snails.

Snails with sauteed notchweeds
(serves 6)

Ingredients
1 kg snails
3 medium-sized potatoes, cut in slices
3 medium-sized courgettes, cut in slices
1 ½ kg notchweeds
2 medium-sized ripe tomatoes, grated
2/3 water glass, olive oil
2 large onions, finely chopped
2 garlic cloves
2 tsp. parsley
salt, pepper

Preparation
Put the snails, onions and garlic in a saucepan and brown them. 5-7 minutes later, add the potatoes and courgettes and when they come to the boil add the notchweeds, which you have previously cleaned and washed very well. When the notchweeds have softened, add the tomatoes, salt, pepper and parsley and cook at low heat for 20 minutes.
Another option is to add a glass of water in the saucepan instead of adding the tomatoes and parsley.

Snails Moussaka
(serves 8)

Ingredients
1 kg long and narrow-shaped aubergines
1 kg medium-sized potatoes,
cut in slices
1 kg snails
3 medium-sized ripe tomatoes, grated
1/4 water glass, olive oil
1 medium-sized onion, finely chopped
salt, pepper

For the bechamel sauce
2 water glasses milk
2 tbsp. corn flour
1 tbsp. fresh butter
some nutmeg
salt
150 gr. yellow cheese, grated

Dissolve the corn flour in some water. Put the milk, butter and corn flour in a casserole, stir them continuously in order for the mixture not to stick and when the sauce becomes thick, add the rest of the ingredients and continue stirring. When the sauce becomes thick, it is ready.

Preparation
The previous night fry the aubergines and potatoes and strain their oil. Prepare the snails (see the other recipes with snails). Take them out of their shell and fry them in the oil for 2 minutes, together with the onion. Add salt, pepper and the tomatoes and cook for 15 minutes. Put a layer of aubergines and potatoes in a baking pan, add half the snails with the tomato sauce and repeat once more. Then cover the food with the bechamel sauce and put it in the oven for one hour, at 200° C.

Snails with spinach
or leeks* (serves 6)

Ingredients
1 kg snails
1 kg spinach or 1 kg leeks
1 medium-sized onion, finely chopped
3 garlic cloves
2/3 water glass, olive oil
½ water glass, white wine
salt, pepper
sauce "Derbille"

Preparation
Put the oil in a saucepan and brown the onion and garlic. Add the snails, cook them for 5-6 minutes and add the wine, salt and pepper. Then add the spinach or leeks and continue cooking for 20-25 minutes, at low heat (if needed add some water). 3 minutes before removing the food from the fire, add the sauce "Derbiye".
Spinach
Wash it well, cut it in big pieces, rub it with coarse salt in order to remove its' water and strain it with your hands.
* Instead of spinach, you can use leeks that you have previously scalded.

Eggs

Eggs with spinach
(serves 4)

Ingredients
300 - 400 gr. spinach leafs
1 medium-sized onion, finely
chopped
½ water glass, olive oil
6 eggs
½ water glass lemon juice
salt

Preparation
Wash the spinach and cut it in
pieces. Brown the onion, and
then add the spinach and cook
until it is soft enough (about 10
minutes). When the spinach is
ready, add salt, beat the 6 eggs
together with the lemon juice,
pour them over the spinach
and cook the food for 2-3
minutes.

Eggs cooked in the ladle

Put some water in a large
and flat ladle and brake
an egg in it. Keep the
ladle over the fire for 2
minutes and your egg is
ready. Of course, you can
only do this in a primus
stove or a liquid

Eggs (omelette) with wild asparagus and avronies (serves 4)

Ingredients

1 kg asparagus and avronies
6 eggs
½ water glass, olive oil
salt, pepper

Preparation

Clean the greens and wash them very well. Cut them in small pieces with your hands, starting from their top where the greens are still tender. Throw away the hard parts. Put the greens in a saucepan, cover them with water and boil for 3-5 minutes. Then strain them and keep ½ water glass of their stock. Put the oil, greens, stock, salt and pepper in a pan and cook them for 3 minutes. Beat the eggs in a bowl and pour them over the greens. Your omelette will be ready in 2 minutes.

Sfougatto (Eggs with courgettes) (serves 4)

Ingredients

5 medium-sized courgettes
1 big ripe tomato, grated
1 onion, finely chopped
½ water glass, olive oil
6 eggs
salt, pepper

Preparation

Wash the courgettes and cut them in small pieces. Put the oil in a pan and when it starts to sizzle, add the onion. When it browns, add the tomato, salt and pepper and cook the food for 5 minutes at low heat. Add the courgettes, continue cooking for 15 minutes and then beat the eggs and add them in the pan, stirring continuously for 2-3 minutes.

Eggs (omelette) with artichokes and tomato* (serves 4)

Ingredients

8 artichokes, cut in four
1 large onion, finely chopped
3/4 water glass, olive oil
2 big ripe tomatoes
4 eggs
1 glass of water
salt, pepper

Preparation

Brown the artichokes and onion
for 5 minutes. Then add the
tomatoes, salt and pepper. Add
the water slowly and cook for
15 minutes at normal heat.
Then beat the eggs, add them in
the pan and continue cooking
for 3-5 minutes.
* This recipe can also be prepared without the artichokes
(only with tomato) following
the same preparation.

Fried eggs with staka

Ingredients
1/4 kg staka
1½ tbsp. flour
4 eggs
salt

Preparation
Put the staka in a frying pan and when it starts to melt, add the flour slowly, stirring continuously until the mixture turns into cream. Then add the eggs, cook for 2-3 minutes and add salt

Fried eggs with water and oil

Put 1/4 glass of water and 1/6 water glass oil in a pan, bring them to the boil them and then add the eggs. Cook for 2 minutes and add some lemon juice.

Potatoes

Porpettes
(potato-croquettes)

Ingredients

½ kg minced meat
5-6 large potatoes
4 eggs
1 tbsp. parsley
salt, pepper, nutmeg
2 tbsp. butter (for browning the minced meat)
1 onion, finely chopped
A handful of grated cheese
200 gr. crushed rusks
olive oil (for frying)

Preparation

Brown the onions and minced meat with the butter. In the mean while, boil the potatoes with their peel, and then peel and mash them. Knead the minced meat and potato mash in a large bowl and add the 3 eggs, parsley, nutmeg, cheese, salt and pepper. Beat 1 egg well. Make small balls, dip them first in the egg then in the rusk, and fry in plenty of olive oil.

Baked potatoes (Oftes)

Ingredients

6-8 medium-sized potatoes
1/4 water glass, olive oil
1/4 water glass lemon juice
salt

Preparation

Wash the potatoes well, dry them, fold
them in aluminium foil and put them in
the oven (180° C) for 1 ½ hour. Then take
them out of the oven, cut them in half and
add some oil, lemon and salt.
In the old days, people used to put the
potatoes (without washing or wrapping
them in anything), in the ashes of either the
oven, fire-place, stove or brazier.
This way they were being cooked by
the heat of the ashes.

Potatoes pasticcio (serves 6)

Ingredients

½ kg minced meat
1 ½ water glass, potato puree (made of 1 ½ kg of potatoes)
3 eggs
1 ½ water glass, grated cheese
salt, pepper
½ water glass, melted fresh butter
2-3 fresh onions
½ tsp. tomato puree
½ water glass crushed rusk
1/3 water glass, olive oil

Preparation

Boil and mash the potatoes. Add the cheese, eggs, salt and pepper.
For the minced meat
Prepare the minced meat the way you prepare it for the spaghetti. Saute the fresh onions in olive oil and before they brown, add the minced meat and brown for 3-4 minutes. Then add water and the tomato-puree and cook the food for 30 minutes. Line a baking pan with butter. Lay half the puree on it, then the minced meat and then the puree again.
Add the rest of the grated cheese, some crushed rusk and the butter. Instead of sprinkling with cheese or rusk, you can prepare bechamel sauce and pour it over the food.

Stuffed potatoes (serves 5)

Ingredients

10 potatoes (thick and medium-sized)
10 small sausages
3 handfuls of grated cheese
3 tbsp. finely chopped parsley
salt, pepper
2 slices of bread, soaked in milk
5 eggs, hard-boiled
1 tbsp. butter
½ water glass, olive oil
2 glasses hot water

For the filling:

Cut the sausages in small pieces, add crumbs from the bread, the egg yolks finely chopped, the cheese, parsley, butter, salt and pepper and knead until the mixture becomes smooth.

Preparation

After peeling the potatoes, put them in a saucepan filled with plenty of water and salt, and boil them (remove from the fire before they become too soft). Let them cool for a while and then make a small hole in each potato and empty it. Fill each potato with the mixture that you have prepared, pour the hot water and olive oil over them and put the food in the oven for about 1 ½ hour, at 180° C. Just before putting the food in the oven, you can sprinkle each potato with some grated cheese.
Instead of sausages, you can use bacon or 3-4 types of cheese.

Potato Pie

Ingredients

640 gr. potatoes, boiled & peeled
640 gr. sugar
320 gr. butter
12 eggs
½ water glass, crushed rusks

Preparation

Boil, peel and mash the potatoes. Beat the eggs well and add them in the potato mash, together with the butter and sugar. Mix them well and pour the mixture in a pan that you have buttered well and sprinkled with crushed rusk. Bake the cake in the oven for about 1 ½ hour, at 180° C.

Potato Cutlets
(serves 4)

Ingredients
4 large potatoes
½ water glass grated cheese
½ water glass crushed rusks
2 eggs
salt, pepper, some cinnamon
olive oil (for frying)

Preparation
Wash the potatoes, cut them in
very thin round slices and
sprinkle with salt, pepper and
cinnamon. Put the eggs and
cheese in a bowl and beat them
well. Put the crushed rusks in
another bowl. Dip the potatoes
first in the eggs and then in the
rusks and fry them in olive oil
at low heat.

Soups

Soup with tahini (serves 5)

Ingredients
450 gr. tahini
(sesame paste)
1 lemon
200 gr. pasta (small)
7 - 9 tbsp. spaghetti
stock

Preparation
Boil the pasta in a big
saucepan. When it is
done, remove from
the fire. Beat the tahini
in the blender and add
the lemon juice slowly.
Using a soup-ladle,
add stock from the
pasta to the mixture, stirring slowly (repeat 7-8
times). Make a smooth thin mixture and add it
slowly in the pasta stirring continuously in order
for the soup not to burn.

Soup with hondro (serves 6)

Ingredients
1/4 kg hondro
2 ripe tomatoes, grated
6 glasses of water (it is better to
use meat broth,
if you have some)
salt

Preparation
Pour the water in a saucepan
and when it comes to the boil,
add the tomatoes and salt and
boil for 10 minutes. Then add
the hondro and continue cooking for 10-15 minutes at low
heat. Serve
with fried bread.

Soups

Pseftosoupa
(serves 4)

Ingredients

2 tbsp. butter made of milk
1 tbsp. flour
boiling water for 4-5 soup plates
4 tbsp. (1 tbsp. for each plate) of sesame-shaped pasta (or
rice for soup)
1 tbsp. olive oil
some lemon juice
salt, pepper, very few cinnamon
1 egg
2 tbsp. flour

Preparation

Boil the water in a saucepan. Put the butter in another casserole and melt it at low heat. When it starts to sizzle, add the flour and stir for 2-3 minutes until it slightly browns. The mixture has to be very thick. Then add the hot water slowly, stirring fast and continuously. The mixture turns into mash and then starts to thin out. After having added all the hot water, add the pasta, olive oil, salt, pepper and cinnamon and cook the food (if you have used rice, cook it a little longer). Beat the eggs in a bowl. Dissolve the flour in the lemon juice and add the mixture in the bowl. Take some broth from the soup, add it in the bowl slowly and prepare the egg-lemon sauce. Remove the soup from the fire and add the egg-lemon sauce stirring continuously so as not to curdle. Your soup is ready!

Tomato-soup
(serves 4)

Ingredients

1 kg ripe tomatoes, grated
½ water glass rice or barley-shaped pasta
2 litres of water
salt
3 potatoes (optional)
2 onions (optional)
2 - 3 carrots (optional)

Preparation

Put the water and tomatoes in a saucepan and boil them for 15 minutes. Then add the salt and rice (or pasta) and continue cooking for 15 more minutes. If you want you can add 3 medium-sized potatoes, 2 onions and some carrots (whole), which you add in the food just before adding the tomato.

Seafood

Fried fish with rosemary
(serves 4)

Ingredients

1 kg red mullet or bogues
olive oil
salt
½ water glass vinegar
1 tsp rosemary
flour

Preparation

Scale, wash, salt and slightly flour the fishes. Put the oil in a frying pan and when it starts to sizzle, fry the fish on both sides for about 15 minutes. Then add the vinegar and rosemary, turn the fish on both sides and remove the pan from the fire.

Seafood

Sea greens, salad

These greens are found in the sea and
you may start picking them in April,
during low tide.
Clean and wash very well and preserve
them in vinegar. When you are about to
eat them, take a serving and pour some
olive oil over it.
It is a fine sour salad, with a strong sea-
flavour. You will mainly find it at the
Kissamos' Province.

Salad with sea-urchins

Ingredients

20-30 sea-urchins*
1 big lemon
3 tbsp. oil

Preparation

Open the sea-urchins and using a tsp.
take their eggs out (they have a bright
dark orange colour). Put the eggs in a
bowl and add the lemon juice and oil.
Add some of the sea water that the
sea- urchins have inside.
*The sea-urchins that are edible
are of brown-red colour and
always have seaweed or a little
stone caught at their quills.

Limpets with spaghetti and basil
(serves 6)

Ingredients

1 soup plate limpets
2 big ripe tomatoes, grated
½ water glass, olive oil
1 tbsp. fresh basil
salt, pepper
1 pack of spaghetti

Preparation

Wash the limpets, scald them and take them out off their shell. Put the oil in a small saucepan, brown the limpets for 12 minutes and then add the tomato, salt and pepper and cook the food for 10-15 minutes. Then add the basil and continue cooking for 10 minutes. Boil the spaghetti, put them in a large flat dish and pour the sauce and limpets over them.

Limpets' pilaff
(serves 6)

Ingredients

40-50 big limpets
3/4 water glass rice
3 ripe tomatoes, grated
1 large onion, finely chopped
½ water glass, olive oil
salt, pepper

Preparation

Wash the limpets well and boil them for 5 minutes. Remove their shells. Put the oil in a saucepan, brown the onions and when they are done, add the limpets and cook them for 2 minutes. Then add the tomatoes, salt and pepper and continue cooking the food for 15 minutes. Add 4 ½ glasses of water and when it comes to the boil, add the rice and continue cooking for 15-20 minutes, stirring in order for the food not to stick.

Shells with red sauce
(serves 6)

Ingredients
1 soup plate shells
1 large onion, finely chopped
1 tsp. parsley
1 tsp. tomato- puree
2/3 water glass, olive oil
½ water glass red wine
salt, pepper
3-4 potatoes (optional)

Preparation
Wash the shells well and take them off their shell, breaking it at the back. Boil them in some water while stirring, for 10 minutes. Strain them and keep their stock. Put the oil in a small saucepan and brown the shells for 1 minute. Then add the parsley, onion, salt and pepper, mix them and add the wine. Then add the tomato-puree and the shells' stock and boil the food until all the water evaporates (for about 20 minutes). If you want, you can add some potatoes cut in thick slices.

Limpets with onions and potatoes
(serves 6)

Ingredients
1 soup plate limpets
1 kg medium-sized potatoes, cut in four
4-5 medium-sized onions, cut in thick slices
2/3 water glass, olive oil
salt

Preparation
Wash the limpets well, scald them and take them off their shell. Put the oil in a saucepan and brown the onions. Add the potatoes, some water and salt and boil the food for 10 minutes. Then add the limpets and continue cooking the food for 10-15 more minutes.

Octopus pilaff
(serves 6)

Ingredients
1 octopus, about 1 ½ kg
1 water glass, red wine
2 medium-sized onions, finely chopped
1 ½ water glass, rice
3 ripe tomatoes
2/3 water glass, olive oil
salt, pepper

Preparation
Put the octopus in a saucepan (without water or oil) and cook it in its' water. When it turns red enough, add the wine, cook for 2-3 minutes, remove from the fire and then cut it into pieces. Brown the onions in a saucepan and then add the octopus. Cook for 2-3 minutes, add the tomatoes, salt and pepper and let it simmer at low heat for 20 minutes. Then add 4 ½ glasses of water and when it comes to the boil, add the rice and cook for 15 minutes, stirring in order for the food not to stick.

Tender octopus (serves 6)

Octopus with artichokes (serves 8)

Ingredients

1 ½ kg octopus
1 tbsp. vinegar
9-10 artichokes
2 lemons cut in half
5 fresh onions, finely chopped
1-2 tbsp. parsley, finely chopped
2 tbsp. dill, finely chopped
2/3 water glass, olive oil
1 big tbsp. flour
salt, pepper

Preparation

Wash the octopus well, put it in saucepan filled with two glasses of water and the vinegar and boil it for 45 minutes -1 hour. Clean the artichokes and put them in a big bowl filled with water and lemon juice. Saute the onions with very little water, add the parsley, dill, oil, salt and pepper and brown them for 2-3 minutes. Cut the octopus in pieces, add it in the saucepan and stir until it browns slightly. Add 1 ½ glass of water and when the food comes to the boil, add the artichokes cut in four (or in half), sprinkle with the flour and cook for 45 minutes.

Ingredients

1.200 gr. octopus
2 medium-sized onions, cut in thick slices
1 ½ water glass red wine
½ water glass, olive oil
salt, pepper, fennel

Preparation

Wash the octopus well and put it in a saucepan (without water or oil). Cook it until all its' water evaporates and then add the wine. 2-3 minutes later, add the oil, onions, salt, pepper and 1 tbsp. finely chopped fennel and simmer the food for 30-40 minutes. If needed, add some water.

Smoked herring with braised rice
(serves 4)

Ingredients

1 herring
1 ½ water glass, rice
2 ripe tomatoes
1 large onion, finely chopped
2/3 water glass, olive oil
salt, pepper

Preparation

Put the oil in a saucepan, brown the onion and then add the tomatoes, salt and pepper and cook the sauce until it thickens (for about 15 minutes). Scale the herring, remove the backbone, cut it in thin slices and add it in the saucepan. Cook the food for 5 minutes and then add 4 ½ glasses of water. When the water comes to the boil, add the rice and continue cooking, stirring from time to time, until the rice is ready (15-20 minutes).

Squid or Octopus with lentils
(serves 6)

Ingredients

1 kg squids or 1 kg octopus
200 gr. lentils
8 fresh onions, finely chopped
1 water glass, olive oil
2 bay leaves
1 big dry onion, grated
300 gr. potatoes cut in big cubes
1 big tomato, finely chopped (or ½ can of finely chopped tomatoes)
1 tbsp. dill, finely chopped
2 tbsp. parsley, finely chopped
1 ½ water glass white wine
salt, pepper

Preparation

Note: for the octopus: Boil it for 45 minutes in 2 glasses of water and ½ water glass vinegar.
Clean the squids and cut them in round slices. Put ½ water glass oil in a saucepan, saute the fresh onions and 1-2 minutes later, add the lentils and cook for about 2 minutes. Add the bay leaves and 1-1/2 glass of water and cook the food for 30 minutes. In the mean while, pour the rest of the oil in another saucepan and saute the onion, squids, potatoes, tomato, parsley and dill at low heat. Then season with salt and pepper, add the wine and simmer the food for 30 minutes. Finally, put the squids and lentils in a large baking pan or a Pyrex dish and bake them in the oven, which you have preheated (200°C), for ½ hour.

Octopus with fresh onions, cooked in wine
(serves 6)

Ingredients

1.200 gr. octopus
2/3 water glass, olive oil
1 water glass red wine
2 tbsp. vinegar
4-5 fresh onions, finely chopped
4 small ripe tomatoes
2 bay leaves
some orange peel
salt, pepper

Preparation

Wash the octopus well, cut it into pieces and cook it in a saucepan without adding water. When all its' water evaporates, add the oil, onions (some of their green part too), salt and pepper, brown them for 5 minutes and then add the wine and vinegar. Three minutes later, add the orange peel, tomatoes, bay leaves and some water (enough to cover the ingredients) and simmer the food at low heat, until it dries of its' water. If the octopus isn't soft enough, add some more water.

Squid casserole (serves 6)

Stuffed squid*
(serves 8)

Ingredients
8 big squids
4 onions, finely chopped
2/3 water glass, olive oil
1 water glass rice
2 lemons
1 tbsp. parsley
salt, pepper

Preparation
Wash the squids well. Remove their gristle, ink, eye gristle and tentacles. Cut the tentacles into pieces and strain them. Put the oil (½ water glass) in a frying pan and when it starts to sizzle, add the onions, brown them and when they are ready, add the rice. Two minutes later add the tentacles, salt, pepper and parsley and brown them for 5-7 minutes. Then add ½ glass of water, cover the pan and simmer the food at low heat until all the water evaporates. Remove the pan from the fire and let the filling cool.
Then stuff the squids with it, using a spoon, and put them in a flat saucepan. Add the rest of the oil, the lemon juice and some water (enough to cover the ingredients) and simmer the food until all its' water evaporates.
* The cuttlefish are being prepared in the same way.

Ingredients
1 kg small squids
1 kg medium-sized potatoes
1 medium-sized onion, finely chopped
2/3 water glass, olive oil
½ kg ripe tomatoes
salt, pepper

Preparation
Clean the squids and wash them well. Put the oil in a saucepan and when it starts to sizzle, add the onion and squids and brown them (3-4 minutes). Then add the tomato, salt and pepper and cook at normal heat for about 1 hour. If needed, add some water.
Twenty minutes before the food is ready, add the potatoes cut in four.

Cuttlefish cooked in wine
(serves 6)

Cuttlefish with fennel and green olives (crushed)
(serves 6)

Ingredients

1 ½ kg cuttlefish, cleaned
2 bunches of fennel, cut in thick pieces
3 large onions, cut in thick slices
1 water glass, red wine
2-3 garlic cloves
500 gr. green olives, crushed
2/3 water glass, olive oil
salt, pepper

Preparation

Remove the stones from the olives and put them in a bowl filled with water in order to soak the extra salt out of them. Wash the cuttlefish well and cut them in stripes. Put the oil in a saucepan and when it starts to sizzle add the onions, cuttlefish and garlic. Brown them, stirring from time to time. When they are ready, add 1½ glass of water, cover the saucepan and cook the food at medium heat. While the cuttlefish are cooking, put the fennel in another saucepan, boil it for a while, strain it and add it in the cuttlefish. Then add the olives, which you have also strained. Season with salt and some pepper and cook the food until the cuttlefish become tender and all the water evaporates.

Ingredients

1 kg cuttlefish
1 onion, finely chopped
1 water glass, olive oil
2/3 water glass red wine
salt, pepper

Preparation

Clean, wash and cut the cuttlefish into pieces. Put the oil in a pan, add the onion, brown it and then add the cuttlefish and cook for 10 minutes. Then season with salt and pepper, add the wine and cook the food at normal heat, for about 45 minutes. If needed, add some water.

Cod-fish with sauteed local greens
(serves 6)

Ingredients

1 kg salted cod-fish
1 kg wild local greens
½ kg spinach
2 large onions, finely chopped
4 garlic cloves
1 water glass, olive oil
2-3 ripe tomatoes, grated
salt, pepper

Preparation

The night before, put the cod-fish in a bowl and cover it with water. Leave it for the night (changing the water 2-3 times) in order for the extra salt to be soaked out of it. Then cut it into pieces. Clean the greens and spinach and wash them well. Put the oil in a saucepan and brown the onions and garlic. Add the greens and spinach slowly and cook them until they soften. Then add the tomatoes, salt and pepper and cook the food at normal heat, for 20 minutes. Ten minutes before you remove the saucepan from the fire, add the pieces of the cod-fish. This dish can be cooked with and without tomatoes.

Braised cuttlefish
(serves 6)

Ingredients
1 kg cuttlefish
2 medium-sized onions, finely chopped
½ water glass wine
3 medium-sized ripe tomatoes, grated
2/3 water glass, olive oil
salt, pepper

Preparation
Clean the cuttlefish, wash them well, cut them into pieces and strain them. Put the oil in a pan, brown the onions and then add the cuttlefish and cook for 3-4 minutes. Add salt, pepper and the wine. Two minutes later, add the tomatoes and cook the food at normal heat for 40-50 minutes. If needed, add some water.

Seafood

Cod-fish casserole (serves 6)

Cod-fish with okra in the oven (serves 6)

Ingredients
1 kg salted cod-fish
1 kg okras, cleaned
5 medium-sized ripe tomatoes, grated
2 onions, finely chopped
1 water glass, olive oil
salt, pepper

Preparation
The night before, cut the cod-fish in pieces, put it in a bowl and cover it with water. Leave it for the night, changing the water 3-4 times, in order for the extra salt to be soaked out. Put the onions and okras in a saucepan, brown them and slowly add some water. Add the tomatoes, salt, and pepper and cook the food for 15-20 minutes. Then pour the food in a large baking pan, lay the pieces of cod-fish on top and cook it in the oven, which you have pre-heated at 180° C, for 20 minutes.

Ingredients
1 kg salted cod-fish
5 large potatoes, cut in big pieces
4 medium-sized ripe tomatoes, grated
2 large onions
2/3 water glass, olive oil
salt, pepper

Preparation
The night before, cut the cod-fish in pieces, put it in a bowl and cover it with water. Leave it for the night, changing the water 3-4 times, in order for the extra salt to be soaked out. Put the onions in a saucepan, brown them and then add the potatoes, tomatoes and salt. Simmer the food at low heat for about 15 minutes. If needed, add some water. Then lay the pieces of the cod-fish on top and continue cooking for 10-12 more minutes. Remove from the fire, add the pepper and the food is ready to be served.

Rice in red sauce with salted cod-fish (serves 6)

Ingredients

1 kg salted cod-fish
1 ½ water glass, rice
2 ripe tomatoes
1 large onion, finely chopped
2/3 water glass, olive oil
salt, pepper

Preparation

Soak the salt out of the cod-fish and bone it. Put the oil in a saucepan and brown the onion. Then add the tomatoes, salt and pepper and cook the food for about 15 minutes, until the sauce thickens. Cut the cod-fish in small slices, add it in the saucepan and cook for 5 minutes. Then add 4 ½ glasses of water and when the food comes to the boil, add the rice and cook it until it is ready, stirring from time to time.

Cod-fish casserole (Stifado) (serves 6)

Ingredients

1 kg salted cod-fish
½ kg medium-sized onions, cut in thick slices
2/3 water glass, olive oil
½ water glass, white wine
salt, pepper
Derbiye sauce

Preparation

The night before, put the cod-fish in a pot and cover it with water. Leave it for the night in order for the extra salt to be soaked out of it and then cut it into pieces. Put the oil in a saucepan and add the onions. Brown, add the wine, salt and pepper and cook for 10-15 minutes (if needed, add some water). Then add the pieces of the cod-fish and continue cooking for 10 minutes. Three minutes before removing the food from the fire, add the sauce Derbiye.

Sauce "Derbiye"

Fill ½ soup plate with lemon juice, add flour, stirring continuously with a fork, and prepare a thin mixture. Then slowly, add 4-6 tbsp. of the food's stock stirring continuously, and when the mixture becomes smooth add it in the food.

Cod-fish with dolmadakia and lettuce leaves
(serves 6)

Ingredients
About 24 fresh lettuce leaves
½ kg salted cod-fish
1 medium-sized onion, grated
4-5 sprigs of celery, finely chopped
½ water glass rice used for soups
½ tsp. Garlic powder
1 tomato, finely chopped
1 can of finely chopped tomatoes
some red cayenne pepper
½ water glass, olive oil
salt, black pepper

Preparation
The night before, put the cod-fish in a bowl and cover it with water. Leave it for the night in order for the extra salt to be soaked out of it. Then remove its' skin and bones and cut it into pieces. Scald the lettuce leaves and let them dry. Mix the rice with the cod-fish, onion, garlic, celery, cayenne pepper and tomato. If needed, add some salt and black pepper. Roll the mixture in lettuce leaves in small portions and make dolmadakia, like you do with the vine leaves. Put them in a saucepan in rows. Pour the tomato can and oil over them. Cover the food with a plate and simmer for about 30 minutes.

Blackfish with okra
(serves 6)

Ingredients
1 ½ kg blackfish, cut in slices
1 kg okra
3 ripe tomatoes, grated
2 large onions, finely chopped
½ water glass, olive oil
salt, pepper

Preparation
Brown the onions and okra and slowly add some water. Add the tomatoes, salt and pepper and cook them for 15-20 minutes. Then put the food in a large baking pan, lay the slices of the fish on top and put it in the oven, which you have pre-heated. Cook for 20 minutes, at 180°C.

Cod-fish barbecue
(serves 6)

Ingredients
1 ½ kg salted cod-fish
the juice of two lemons
olive oil
1 lemon cut in half
salt

Preparation
The night before, cut the cod-fish in pieces, put it in a bowl and cover it with water. Leave it for the night in order for the extra salt to be soaked out. Put the lemon juice, oil and salt in a bowl and mix them. Dip the pieces of the cod-fish in the bowl and then broil them. Glaze the broiler with oil and heat it in the fire, in order for the cod-fish not to stick on it. Use the lemon to glaze the cod-fish continuously.

Bonito in pickling-brine*
(serves 4)

Ingredients
1 big bonito
3-4 lemons
½ water glass parsley, finely chopped
pepper (15 seeds)
3 cloves
4-5 bay leaves
orange peel, cut in slices
vinegar

Preparation
Wash the fish well, scale it and remove its' head. Put it in a deep bowl, which you have filled with strong pickling-brine (salt water that will completely cover the fish). In the pickling- brine you must also add the lemon juice, parsley, pepper, cloves, orange peel, bay leaves and some vinegar. Soak the fish in it for 2 ½ hours, then take it out, cut it in slices and preserve it in the oil.

* This is the traditional recipe of all the poor people in the world. It can be found in slight variations, according to the climate of each country. In South America (Peru), the same recipe is called Sevitche. Of course, this recipe can be prepared with any kind of fat fish (pagrus, etc.) "Cooked" in pickling-brine, it is a first-class snack.

Baked bonito (in the oven or in the saucepan)
(serves 6)

Ingredients
1 bonito, 1 ½ kg, cut in slices
½ kg onions
2 tbsp. parsley
3 ripe tomatoes, grated
2/3 water glass, olive oil
salt, pepper

Preparation
Cut the onions in thin slices and brown them in the oil. Then add the tomatoes, salt, pepper and parsley and cook the food for about 15 minutes. Then put the bonito slices in the saucepan and continue cooking the food at low heat for 15 more minutes. If needed, add some water.
The same food can also be cooked in the oven, at 180° C. In that case, you have to previously cook the sauce in a saucepan.

The fisherman's soup
(serves 6)

Ingredients

1 - 1 ½ kg rock fishes (scorpion-fishes,
perches, wrasses, cod-fish, etc.)
1-2 garlic cloves
½ water glass, ouzo or tsipouro or tsikoudia
salt, pepper

Preparation

Take the fish and clean them very well.
Put them inside the jaconet, add the garlic, sprinkle with the ouzo and close the
jaconet well, tying it tight. Put the
jaconet in a saucepan and add water until
the bundle is almost covered. In the old
times, the fishermen used sea water to
make this soup, because they cooked it
on their boats.
Add salt and boil the food for 1 hour.
Remove from the fire and take the
jaconet off the pan. Serve the broth in
cups and the fish in a large flat dish,
together with the jackonet. You can add
some pepper if you want.

Kakavia (fish-soup)
(serves 6)

Ingredients

1 ½ kg various fishes *
(small scorpion-fishes, combers,
cod-fishes, etc.)
½ water glass, olive oil
1 big ripe tomato
2 big potatoes
2 small onions
½ water glass lemon juice
salt, pepper

Preparation

Clean the fish and wash them well. Put
water in a saucepan, seeing that it is
enough to cover the fishes. Bring it to
the boil, add the oil, tomato, potatoes,
onions (all cut in four) and salt and boil
the food for 10 minutes at normal heat.
Then add the fish (according to size),
continue cooking for 10 more minutes
and before removing the pan from the
fire, add the pepper and lemon juice.
In old times, the people used to cook
kakavia on their boats, using sea water.
You can also use shell-fish.

Fish soup
(serves 6)

Ingredients

1 ½ kg fish (suitable for soup)
3 large potatoes, cut in thick slices
4-5 carrots
3-4 sprigs of celery
1/3 water glass, olive oil
1/4 kg rice suitable for soups
1 egg
1 lemon
salt

Preparation

Put water in a saucepan, add salt and
when it boils, add the potatoes, carrots
and celery and boil them for 20 minutes.
Add the fish, continue cooking for about
15 minutes and then empty the saucepan
and strain the fish broth. Take half of the
fish and the vegetables and mash them.
Take the broth, oil, mashed vegetables
and fishes and some salt, put them in the
pan again and when they start boiling,
add the rice and cook for 20 minutes.
Prepare the egg-lemon sauce, add it in
the food, mix and your soup is ready.

Sardines in the oven
(serves 4)

Ingredients

1 kg medium to large-sized sardines
1/4 water glass, olive oil
1/4 water glass lemon juice
salt, oregano

Preparation

Scale the sardines, wash them well, salt them, put them in a baking pan in two layers, season with the oil and lemon juice, sprinkle with some oregano and bake them at medium heat, at 180° C,for 20-30 minutes.

Sardines with vine leaves
(serves 4)

Ingredients

1 kg sardines, cleaned (without their heads),
washed and strained well
1/4 water glass, olive oil
juice of 1 lemon
2 lemons cut in slices
100 gr. vine leaves
salt, pepper
oregano

Preparation

Season the sardines with salt and pepper. Mix half the oil with the lemon juice and pour it over the sardines. Cover the bottom of a medium-sized baking pan with vine leaves, put a layer of sardines over them and then add oregano and 2-4 lemon slices. Then cover with vine leaves again, put a layer of sardines on top, add oregano and 4-5 lemon slices and cover with vine leaves once more. Pour the rest of the oil over the food, lay the rest of the lemon slices on top and bake it in the oven (which you have pre-heated) for about ½ hour, at 220° C.

Salad with sardines

Ingredients

8-9 sardines
1 slice of bread
1 boiled egg
2 raw egg yolks
1 lemon
olive oil
mustard

Preparation

Take 8-9 sardines and soak them in water for 1 hour. Then bone them and pound them in a wooden mortar. Soak a slice of bread in water and pound it. Take the yolk off the boiled egg, put it in the bowl where you will prepare the salad and mix it until it becomes a mash. Put the sardines in the bowl and mix them well with some lemon, the bread and the two raw egg yolks. Then add some oil and lemon juice and mix the ingredients until they turn into paste. Finally, add some mustard.

Salted Sardines

Wash the sardines and then put them in a pot. Put a layer of sardines first and then a layer of salt. Continue the procedure until the pot is full and leave them there for 15 days. Then, remove their entrails, wash them with plenty of water and finally, with water and vinegar. Strain them and put them in a pot, adding cloves, ground pepper and bay leaves. Cover them with oil and leave them for 15 days.

Fresh Sardines

Take the sardines, remove their heads and entrails, wash them well and then put them in a strainer. Let them strain and then salt them. In the mean while, put water in a saucepan. When it comes to the boil, put the strainer in the saucepan and boil the sardines for 10 minutes, seeing that they are well covered by water. Then take the strainer out of the casserole, strain the sardines, put them in a pot and cover them with oil. They will become even tastier if you also cover them with caper.

Meat

Lamb or Goat with avronies and asparagus (wild asparagus)* (serves 6)

Ingredients
1200 gr. lamb or kid
1 ½ kg avronies and asparagus
1 water-glass, olive oil
salt, pepper

Preparation
Clean and wash the greens well, boil them for 10 minutes in very hot water and strain them. Wash the meat, cut it into pieces, season with salt and pepper and brown it on both sides for 5-7 minutes. Then add 1 to 1 ½ glass of water slowly, and cook at low heat until the food is ready. Ten minutes before removing the saucepan from the fire, add some water and the greens and continue cooking for 2-3 minutes.
* The asparagus are being used so as to temper the bitterness of the avronies.
* If you want, you can add egg-lemon sauce.

Meat casserole or sauteed meat* from Sfakia (Tsigariasto) (serves 6)

Ingredients
1 ½ kg zigouri (the front part, not the leg)
2 water glasses, olive oil
salt, pepper

Preparation
Wash the meat well, cut it in small pieces, put it in a big bowl and let it dry for 2-3 hours. Put the oil in a saucepan and before it starts to sizzle, add the meat and cook it in very high heat, stirring continuously, until it turns white. Then season with salt and pepper, cover the casserole, lower the fire to half and cook the food for 1 ½ -2 ½ hours. Attention: Do not add water. You must serve the meat almost dry, not floating in oil.
* In the area of Sfakia, instead of zigouri, they use agrimi or fouriariko, that is, goats that have grazed out in the open. These animals are characteristic for their good taste and dark coloured meat.

Lamb with staka in the oven
(serves 6)

Ingredients
1 - 1 ½ kg leg of lamb
300 - 500 gr. staka
salt, pepper, plenty of oregano

Preparation
Season the meat with salt and pepper, add the oregano, put it in a greaseproof paper and glaze with the staka. Close the greaseproof paper well and roast the food in the oven for 2 hours, at 180° C.

Lamb with yoghurt
(serves 6)

Ingredients
1 ½ kg lamb
2-4 eggs
2 tbsp. fresh butter, melted
1 kg strained yoghurt
salt, pepper

Preparation
Boil the lamb (for about 45 minutes), bone it and season with salt and pepper. Then put it in a baking pan, beat the eggs with the yoghurt, glaze the meat with this mixture and leave it for one hour. Before putting it in the oven, pour the butter over it and bake (at normal heat) for 15 to 20 minutes.

Lamb with wild artichokes
(serves 6)

Ingredients
1 kg lamb
1 kg wild artichokes
3 medium-sized ripe tomatoes, grated
3/4 water-glass, olive oil
salt, pepper

Preparation
Put the oil in a saucepan, add the meat and brown it. Add salt, pepper and the tomatoes and cook for about 45 minutes. If needed add some water. Clean and wash the artichokes, boil them for 15 minutes and strain them. Take the meat off the sauce, add the artichokes, boil them for 10 minutes and then add the meat and continue cooking the food for about 10 minutes.
If you want you can add egg-lemon sauce instead of tomatoes.

Lamb or Goat with artichokes
(serves 6)

Ingredients
1.200 gr. lamb or kid
10 artichokes
1 big ripe tomato, grated
1 onion, finely chopped
1 glass of water
2/3 water-glass, olive oil
salt, pepper

Preparation
Wash the lamb well and cut it into portions. Put the oil in a saucepan and when it starts to sizzle, add the meat, onion, salt and pepper. Brown the meat on all sides then add the tomato and water and simmer for approximately one hour, at low heat. Cut the artichokes in four, add them in the saucepan and continue boiling for 10 more minutes.

Lamb or Goat with stamnagkathi or chicory, with egg-lemon sauce

(serves 6)

Ingredients

1.200 gr. lamb or kid
1 ½ kg stamnagkathi or chicory
2/3 water glass, olive oil
salt, pepper
For the egg-lemon sauce
1-2 eggs
½ water glass lemon juice

Preparation

Clean and wash the greens well. Boil them
for 15 minutes in very hot water and then
strain them. Wash and cut the meat into
pieces. Season with salt and pepper and
brown on all sides for 5-7 minutes. Then
add 1 to 1 ½ glasses of water slowly, and
cook until the food is ready (1 to 1 ½ hour).
Ten minutes before the meat is done, add a
glass of water and the greens and continue
cooking. Then turn off the heat, prepare the
egg-lemon sauce, then stir continuously
while pouring the sauce so as not to curdle.
This food can also be prepared without the
egg-lemon sauce. In this case, do not add
the last glass of water in the saucepan.

Roast lamb heads with pasta and tomatoes (Giouvetsi) (serves 4)

Ingredients
2 lamb heads cut in half
3 medium-sized ripe tomatoes, grated
½ kg barley-shaped pasta (kritharaki)
½ water glass, olive oil
salt, pepper
½ water glass vinegar
4-5 water glasses broth

Preparation
Fill a bowl with cold water, add ½ water glass vinegar, put the heads inside, soak them for 2 hours and then wash them. Fill a saucepan with plenty of water, add some salt, boil the heads for ½ hour and then skim them. Take them out of the saucepan, keep 5 water glasses of their broth and put them in a baking pan. Add the oil, pepper, tomatoes and a water glass of broth and put them in the oven for 45 minutes, at 180° C. Then add 3 to 3 ½ water glasses broth and when the food comes to the boil, add the pasta and cook for 15-17 minutes. If needed, add some more broth.

Lamb heads with potatoes in the oven (serves 4)

Ingredients
2 lamb heads cut in half
3 ripe tomatoes, grated
½ water glass, olive oil
1 kg potatoes, cut in thick slices
salt, pepper
1 water glass broth

Preparation
Wash the heads well, fill a saucepan with plenty of water, add salt and boil them for ½ hour. Keep a water glass of their broth. Put them in a baking pan, add the potatoes, tomatoes, oil, salt, pepper and broth and put the food in the oven for 1 ½ hour, at 180° C.

Soup with lamb head and kritharaki (serves 4)

Ingredients
2 lamb heads cut in half
1/3 water glass, olive oil
2 ripe tomatoes, grated
1/4 kg barley-shaped pasta (kritharaki)
salt

Preparation
Wash the heads well, cut them in half, season with plenty of salt and boil them in plenty of water for 1 ½ to 2 hours, at normal heat. When they are ready, strain their broth and put them in a large flat dish. Put the broth in a saucepan, add the oil, tomatoes and some salt, if needed, and when the food comes to the boil twice, add the pasta and cook for 15-20 minutes.

Lamb pie (area of Kidonia) (serves 6)

Ingredients

1 ½ kg baby lamb
850 gr. flour
1 kg sweet mizithra
½ kg staka
1 egg
1 yoghurt-cup
250 gr. fresh butter
salt, pepper, sesame

Preparation

Wash the meat and boil it in water for 1 to 1 ½ hour. Bone it, put the meat in a large flat dish and season with salt and pepper. Prepare the dough using the flour, yoghurt and butter. Roll out a pastry sheet (½ cm thick), put it in a baking pan and line it with butter. Pour a layer of mizithra and half the staka over it. Put the meat on the mizithra, lay the rest of the mizithra and staka over it and cover with a second pastry sheet. Press the pastry sheets' ends together, in order for the filling not to spill during baking, glaze the pastry sheet with egg yolk, sprinkle with sesame and roast the food for about 1 hour at 180° C.

Lamb pie (serves 6)

Ingredients

1.200 gr. baby lamb
½ kg mizithra
5 boiled eggs cut in four, alongside
3 eggs (raw)
½ water-glass, olive oil
salt, pepper

Preparation

Wash the lamb well and boil it in water. When it is ready, bone it and season with salt and pepper. Put the 3 raw eggs, oil and meat in a large bowl and mix them. Roll out a pastry sheet, line it with oil, put it in a baking pan, pour the mixture over it and cover with the boiled eggs. Cover the food with another pastry sheet, close its' ends well and roast it at 180°C for 45 minutes.

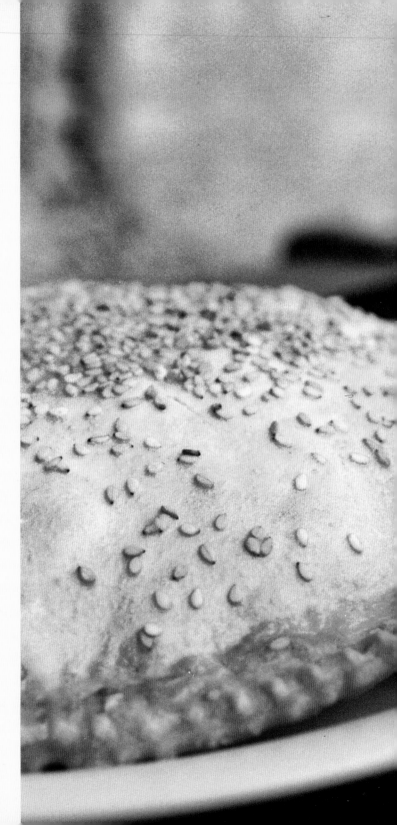

Stuffed spleens (A) (serves 6)

Ingredients
4-5 medium-sized lamb
spleens
200 gr. minced- lamb meat
(with its' fat)
salt, pepper, cinnamon,
oregano, parsley
1 small onion, finely
chopped
½ water glass wine
½ water glass, olive oil (for
frying)

Preparation
Wash the spleens and carve
them in the middle. Put the
minced-meat, onion,
flavourings, salt and pepper
in a bowl and mix them. Fill
the spleens with the mixture,
sew them and fry them in
sizzling oil on both sides. 5
minutes later, add ½ water
glass red wine, lower the heat
and simmer the food until
only the oil remains.

Stuffed spleens (B) (serves 6)

Ingredients
4 lamb spleens (not very
small)
2 eggs
salt, pepper, parsley
50 gr. bolia (or skepi)
garlic (optional)

Preparation
Carve the spleens alongside,
paying attention not to cut
them in half. Boil the 2 eggs,
remove almost half of their
white and cut the rest in
small pieces. Finely chop the
parsley, bolia (fat) and garlic
(if you use it). Mix them
with the eggs, fill the spleens
with the mixture, sew them
and fry them in oil for 10-15
minutes.

Soup
with goat meat and
kritharaki
(serves 6)

Ingredients
1.200 gr. goat meat
1/3 water glass, olive oil
2 ripe tomatoes, grated
1/4 kg. barley-shaped pasta (kritharaki)
salt

Preparation
Wash the meat well, cut it into pieces, season with plenty of salt and boil it in plenty of water for 1 ½ to 2 hours, at normal heat. When it is ready, strain the broth and put the meat in a large flat dish. Put the broth in a saucepan, add the oil, tomatoes and some salt, if needed, bring it to the boil twice, and then add the kritharaki and cook for 15-20 minutes.

Boiled zigouri, pilaff
(serves 6)

Ingredients
1.200 gr. zigouri
2 water glasses, rice (not granular)
6 water glasses, broth
2 tbsp. butter made of staka
salt
½ water glass, lemon juice

Preparation
Wash the meat well, put it in a saucepan,
add water and 1 tbsp. salt and boil at low
heat for at least 1 ½ hour. When it is
ready, take it out of the saucepan and
strain its' broth. Put the broth in a
saucepan, bring it to the boil, add the rice,
stirring continuously in order for the food
not to stick, and cook until there is no
more broth left (about 20 minutes). Sizzle
the butter in a coffee-pot, pour it over the
pilaff and leave it covered for 5 minutes.
Serve the rice and meat separately.
If you want, you can add 1/4 water glass
lemon juice in the rice, five minutes before it
is ready (and before adding the butter).

Pork
with celery
(serves 6)

Ingredients

1 kg pork (boneless)
1½ kg celery
4 medium-sized ripe tomatoes
1 onion
1 water glass, olive oil
salt, pepper

Preparation

Clean the celery, wash it well and scald it (boil it for 10 minutes and then strain it). Put the oil in a saucepan and when it starts to sizzle, add the meat, salt, pepper and onion and brown them for 10 minutes. Then add the tomatoes and cook the food for about 45 minutes at normal heat. Finally, add the celery and continue cooking for 20 minutes.

Braised pork meat
(serves 6)

Ingredients
1.200 gr. lean boneless pork meat
½ water glass, olive oil
3 ripe tomatoes
1 large onion
½ water glass red wine
salt, pepper

Preparation
Wash the meat and cut it in portions. Brown the onion in a saucepan, add the meat and brown it for 3-4 minutes on both sides. Add salt, pepper and the wine and 2 minutes later, add the tomatoes and cook the food at low heat for one hour. If needed, add some water.

Baby pork with petimezi (grape-juice syrup) (serves 6)

Ingredients

1/4 water glass, olive oil
1 ½ kg leg of pork with its' skin (baby pork)
2-3 large onions, cut in thick slices
3 garlic cloves
½ water glass red wine
1/4 water glass petimezi (grape-juice syrup)
½ kg potatoes, cut in cubes
salt, pepper, cinnamon, oregano

Preparation

Prepare the marinade using the petimezi, a bit of oil (2 - 3 tbsp.), the oregano and a pinch of cinnamon. Marinate the meat for one night (do not throw away the marinade). Put the oil in a saucepan and when it starts to sizzle, add the onions, garlic and pork. Brown them, add the wine and marinade and simmer for about 30 minutes. You might need to add some water (1 glass). Add the potatoes, salt and pepper, put the meat in a baking pan and put it in the oven, which you have pre-heated at 150° C. Add 1 ½ glass of water, season with some salt, pepper and cinnamon and roast until the potatoes are ready (for about 20 minutes).

Omates (stuffed pork bowel)

Christmas snack of the mountain areas of the Chania Prefecture Wash the bowel or intestines very well and soak them for two hours in lemon juice, where you have added lemon or bitter orange peel. Put rice, raisins, salt, pepper and cumin in a bowl, mix them and fill the bowel or intestines with the mixture. When the bowel is full, tie its' ends and sprinkle with cinnamon. Then boil it for 1 hour. You can also cook pork trotters in the same way. Remove the main (central) bone, fill them with the mixture, tight them, sprinkle with some oil and thyme and put them in the oven for about 2 hours.

Apakia

Apakia are made of lean boneless pork meat. They are stripes of pork meat (2-3 cm) taken from the area around the kidneys, which is the most tasty part of the animal. They are of dark purple colour and have been smoked at the fire -usually at the fireplace- together with herbs. Smoking is a very old way of preserving meat. It is being used since the ancient times. Apakia are a tasty snack, ideal for accompanying ouzo and wine. They are quite heavy to be eaten as a main course.

Siglina

Remove the fat from the pork meat, keep it and cut the rest in stripes (3-5 cm). Sprinkle the stripes with sage, pepper and cumin, lay them inside a wooden mesh and salt them well. Keep the mesh over the fireplace, seeing that it is far enough from the fire. Put various spices in the fireplace (thyme, sage, oregano, etc.) and smoke the meat for a whole day. Then wash it very well (with green soap), cut it in mouthfuls, sprinkle with pepper, oregano and cumin and brown it in the fat that you have kept.

You can keep the meat in the pork fat for as long as you wish. When you are about to serve it, heat it in a frying pan, using some of its' fat.

(Tsigarides: it is the pork fat that you cut in small pieces, fry it and preserve in the siglina).

Ways of serving:
a) Fried in their fat
b) In red sauce, served with fried potatoes
c) Roast meat with barley-shaped pasta and tomatoes, cooked in the oven or in the casserole

Roast pork meat with barley-shaped pasta and tomatoes (Giouvetsi)
(serves 6)

Ingredients
1.200 gr. lean boneless pork meat*
½ water glass, olive oil
½ kg barley-shaped pasta (kritharaki)
3 ripe tomatoes, chopped very finely
salt, pepper

Preparation
Wash the meat, cut it into portions and put it in a baking pan. Add the oil, salt, pepper, tomatoes and ½ glass of water and roast the food for one hour, at 200°C. Then add two glasses of water and when the food comes to the boil, add the pasta and continue cooking for 20 more minutes. If needed, add some water.

* Instead of lean boneless pork meat you can use pork cutlets.

Meat

Tzoulamas*
(serves 6)

Ingredients

½ kilo pork liver, cut to bite-sized pieces
½ kilo rice (short-grained, white)
½ cup sugar
1 cup currants
1 cup almonds, finely-chopped
½ cup olive oil
½ teaspoon cinnamon
½ kilo phyllo pastry
Salt and pepper to taste

Preparation

Heat the oil in a pan, add the liver and
cook for 2-3 minutes. Season with salt and
pepper, pour in 2-3 cups of water, bring to
boil and add the rice. 20 minutes later,
remove from heat and add the almonds,
currants, sugar and mix well. Oil a baking
pan and lay 3 pastry sheets. Spread out the
prepared mixture on top and cover with
the rest 3 pastry sheets. Top with sugar and
cinnamon, sprinkle with water and brush
the surface with oil. Bake in the oven for
30-40 minutes, at 180oC.

* Tzoulamas: Cretan meat pie of Crete,
traditionally baked during carnival, which is
stuffed with pork liver, rice, currants and
almonds and is sprinkled with sugar and
cinnamon

Roast meat wrapped in paper
(serves 6)

Ingredients

1 kg pork meat
4 garlic cloves
3-4 onions, finely chopped
2 tbsp. parsley, finely chopped
1 ½ tbsp. fresh butter
8 lemon slices
salt, pepper, oregano

Preparation

Cut the meat in 3-4 pieces and add the garlic, oregano, onions, parsley, lemon slices, butter, salt and pepper. Wrap it in 2-3 greaseproof papers and roast it in the oven at 180°C for about 2 hours.

Pork with chickpeas
(serves 6)

Ingredients

1 kilo pork, boneless
1 large onion, finely chopped
4-5 medium-sized, ripe tomatoes
½ kilo chickpeas
1 cup olive oil
Salt - pepper

Preparation

Soften the chickpeas by soaking overnight in tepid water to soften. In a pot heat the oil, add the onion and saute. Cut the pork into portions and add to the pot, season with salt and pepper and mix. Cook for 2-3 minutes and add the grated tomatoes. Simmer for another 20-35 minutes. Subsequently, combine with the chickpeas, pour in 2 cups of water and let simmer for 20 minutes. If necessary, add some more water.

Pork soup with frumenty and noodles (Chilopites)
(serves 8)

Ingredients

2 kg pork meat (preferably from the head or with bones and fat)
2 water glasses frumenty (crushed wheat boiled in milk and then dried)
2 water glasses noodles (Chilopites)
3-4 lemons
salt, pepper

Preparation

Boil the pork in plenty of water until it almost melts. Take it out of the saucepan and season with plenty of salt. Strain the broth and keep 2 water glasses of broth for each portion that you want to cook. Put the broth in a saucepan, add the meat, frumenty, noodles, salt and pepper and boil for about 20 minutes at low heat. Five minutes before removing the food from the fire, add the lemon juice. Serve with rusk (which you add in the saucepan) and extra lemon (if you so prefer).

Pork- head (pork-jelly)

Ingredients
1 small pork head (up to 2 kg)
2-3 carrots
2-3 sprigs of celery
2-3 cloves
2 bay leaves
vinegar, lemon
salt, roughly ground pepper

Preparation
Wash the head well and soak it in cold water for 2-3 hours. Start boiling it in water, skim it, add the carrots, celery and flavourings and continue boiling it for about 1 ½ hour. Then strain its' broth, add 2-3 tbsp. vinegar or a tbsp. lemon juice in it and continue boiling the food at low heat. Boil the broth until there is enough left to cover the head's meat. When the head cools, bone it, cut the meat in small pieces, add plenty of salt and pepper, put it in a form, pour the rest of the broth over it and leave it cool.

Kilidakia (gardoumakia) with tomato (serves 6)

Ingredients
2 small lamb-stomachs with their intestines
4 lamb trotters
½ water glass, olive oil
1 medium- sized onion, finely chopped
salt, pepper
4-5 lemons
2 big ripe tomatoes
3-4 potatoes, cut in four
½ kg courgettes, cut in half

Preparation
Wash the entrails and trotters very well and put them in a bowl half filled with water, together with 4-5 lemons cut in four. Soak them for 2 hours and then scald them, cut the stomachs in long and narrow pieces (10-15 cm) and roll the intestines around them. Do the same with the trotters. Put them in a saucepan filled with water, bring them to the boil (7-10 minutes), take them out and throw away the water. Put the oil, onion, salt, pepper, gardoumakia (meat) and tomatoes in a saucepan, cover them with water and boil for 50 minutes. Then add the potatoes and courgettes and cook the food at low heat for about 20 minutes.

Kilidakia (gardoumakia) with egg-lemon sauce (serves 6)

Ingredients
2 small lamb-stomachs with their intestines
4 lamb trotters
½ water glass, olive oil
1 medium- sized onion, finely chopped
2 eggs
½ water glass lemon juice
salt, pepper
4-5 lemons

Preparation
Wash the entrails and trotters very well and put them in a bowl half filled with water, together with 4-5 lemons cut in four. Soak them for 2 hours and then scald them, cut the stomachs in long and narrow pieces (10-15 cm) and roll the intestines around them. Do the same with the trotters. Put them in a saucepan filled with water, bring them to the boil (7-10 minutes), take them out and throw away the water. Put the oil, onion, gardoumbakia (meat), salt and pepper in a saucepan and cover them with water. Boil at low heat for 1 hour and 15 minutes. Then turn off the heat, prepare the egg-lemon sauce and add it in the food, stirring continuously.

For the egg-lemon sauce
Put the egg whites in a bowl, beat them to a meringue and then add the yolks and continue beating. Using a ladle, take some broth from the saucepan and add it in the bowl slowly, together with the lemon juice, stirring continuously in order for the egg not to turn (repeat 4-5 times). After having poured enough broth in it and when the mixture is warm enough , add it in the saucepan and mix with the food.

Rabbit

Braised rabbit cooked in wine (serves 6)

Ingredients
1 rabbit, about 1.200 gr.
1 water glass, red wine
2 onions
2/3 water glass, olive oil
3-4 medium-sized ripe tomatoes, grated
salt, pepper

Preparation
Wash the rabbit well, cut it into portions and strain it for one hour. Put the oil in a saucepan and when it starts to sizzle, add the rabbit and brown it on both sides. Then cut the onions in thin slices, add them in the casserole and 2 minutes later, add the wine. When the wine evaporates (3 minutes later), add the tomatoes, salt and pepper, lower the fire to half and simmer for about 45 minutes.

Rabbit casserole (Stifado) (serves 6)

Ingredients
1 rabbit, about 1.200 gr.
2/3 water glass, olive oil
1 kg small onions (for stew)
4 medium-sized ripe tomatoes, grated
1 orange peel
½ water glass red wine
salt, pepper, clove, cinnamon, pimento, bay leaves

Preparation
Wash the rabbit well and cut it into portions. Put the oil in a saucepan and when it starts to sizzle, add the rabbit and brown it well on both sides. Then add salt, pepper and the wine. Cook until it comes to the boil twice (about 5 minutes), add the onions and cook for 5-10 minutes. Then add the tomatoes and a glass of water, lower the fire below normal and cook for 45 minutes. Five minutes before removing the saucepan from the fire, add the orange peel and flavourings. Attention: Do not stir the food during cooking, in order for the onions not to melt.

Rabbit with potatoes in the oven (cooked in lemon juice or red sauce) (serves 6)

Fried rabbit
(serves 6)

Ingredients
1 rabbit, about 1.200 gr.
1 water glass, red wine or 1/3 water glass, vinegar
½ water glass, olive oil
salt, pepper

Preparation
Wash the rabbit well, cut it into portions, season with salt and pepper, put it in a bowl filled with the wine or vinegar and leave it for 2-3 hours. Put the oil in a saucepan and when it starts to sizzle, add the rabbit and brown it at high heat for ½ hour. Then lower the heat and simmer for about 20 minutes (if needed add some water). Before serving, put a layer of lemon leaves in a large flat dish, put the rabbit on it and cover for 10 minutes.

Ingredients
1 rabbit, about 1.200 gr.
1 kg potatoes
the juice of two medium-sized lemons
2/3 water glass, olive oil
3 medium-sized ripe tomatoes, grated
salt, pepper, oregano

Preparation
Wash the rabbit well, cut it into portions, put it in a baking pan and add the potatoes. Add salt, pepper, the oil and a glass of water. If you want it cooked in lemon juice, add the lemon juice and oregano. If you want it cooked in red sauce, add the tomatoes. Cook it in the oven for 60-75 minutes, at 200° C.

Rabbit stuffed with mizithra or staka (serves 6)

Rabbit cooked in lemon juice with thyme or oregano (serves 6)

Ingredients

1 rabbit, about 1.200 gr.
2/3 water glass, olive oil
1 large onion, finely chopped
juice of three medium-sized lemons
1 tbsp. thyme or 1 tsp. oregano
salt, pepper

Preparation

Wash the rabbit well and cut it into portions. Put the oil in a saucepan and when it starts to sizzle, add the onion and brown it. Add the rabbit and brown it on both sides for 5-7 minutes. Then add salt, pepper, thyme or oregano, the lemon juice and a glass of water and simmer the food for 40 minutes at normal heat. If its' water evaporates during cooking, you can add some more.

Ingredients

1 rabbit, about 1.200 gr.
200 gr. mizithra or staka
1 big lemon
salt, pepper

Preparation

Wash the rabbit well, stuff it with the staka or mizithra and sew it in order for the filling not to slop over. Then put it in a baking pan, add salt and pepper, pour the lemon juice over it and put it in the oven at 180° C, for about 2 hours.

Marinade for hare or rabbit

Ingredients

1 ½ water glass black dry wine
½ water glass strong vinegar or red wine
1/8 water glass oil
2 medium-sized onions cut in thin slices
2 big garlic loves, pounded
1 tbsp. thyme
a little bunch of rosemary
5 bay leaves
up to 15 grains roughly grounded pepper

Preparation

Put all the ingredients in a big glass bowl and mix them very well.
Cut the hare (or rabbit) in medium-sized pieces (not big) and soak them in the marinade for 12 hours. The meat has to be covered by the sauce, therefore it mustn't weight more than 2 kilos.

Hare (or rabbit) with garlic sauce (serves 8)

Ingredients

1 hare or 1 rabbit, about 2 kg
½ water glass oil
1 ½ water glass red wine
6-7 garlic cloves (whole)
4-5 garlic cloves (pounded)
2 medium-sized onions
2-3 bay leaves
salt, pepper
1 ½ water glass red wine

For the sauce
1-2 tbsp. flour
some salt

Preparation

The previous day, put the hare or rabbit (whole or cut in portions) in a bowl filled with the wine. Clean 6-7 garlic cloves, put them inside the hare's skin and soak it in the wine during the whole night. The following day, put the hare or rabbit in a saucepan, add the wine, onion, pounded garlic cloves, bay leaves and oil and brown the food for 3-4 minutes. Add 1 ½ water glass wine, cover the food with a plate, cover the casserole and simmer at low heat for 1 ½ -2 hours.
Prepare the sauce: When the food is ready, remove the hare from the saucepan and put it in a large flat dish.
Pour the flour in the saucepan, add some salt, if needed, mix well and bring the mixture to the boil until the sauce becomes quite thick. Pour it over the hare or rabbit.

Poultry

Chicken with chestnuts (in white or red sauce) (serves 6)

Ingredients
1 chicken, 1 ½ kg
2 medium-sized onions
1 red pepper
2 kg chestnuts, boiled and peeled
½ water glass, olive oil
½ water glass red wine
salt, pepper

Preparation
Wash the chicken, cut it into portions, add salt and pepper, brown it in oil for 10 minutes and then add the wine. Cut the onions and pepper in small pieces and add them in the saucepan. Brown them for 2-3 minutes, add some water and cook the food at normal heat for 30'. Then add the chestnuts and cook for 10 more minutes. If you want, you can add two grated ripe tomatoes instead of water.

Hen giblets omelette (serves 4)

Ingredients
½ kg giblets
4 eggs
salt, pepper
½ water glass, olive oil
(for frying)

Preparation
Wash the giblets well, cut them in small pieces and add salt and pepper. Put the oil in a frying pan and when it starts to sizzle, add the giblets and cook them for 7 minutes on both sides. A few minutes before removing the food from the fire, beat the eggs and add them in the pan.

Hen and Zigouri* pilaff
(serves 8)

Ingredients
1 kg zigouri (*two-year-old lamb)
1 hen, weighting 1 ½ kg)
2 water glasses rice (not granular)*
6 water glasses broth
2 tbsp. butter made of staka
1/4 water glass lemon juice
salt

Preparation
Wash the meat well. Fill a saucepan with water, add
a tbsp. salt and boil the meat at low heat for at least
1 ½ hour. When it is ready, take it out and strain its'
broth. Put the broth in a saucepan, boil it, add the
rice and cook for about 20 minutes (until all the
water evaporates), stirring continuously in order for
the food to stick. Sizzle the butter in a coffee-pot,
pour it over the pilaff and leave it covered for 5
minutes. Serve the rice and meat separately.
If you want, five minutes before the rice is done (and
before adding the butter), you can add ? water glass
lemon juice in the casserole.

Cretan pilaff with rooster or hen
(serves 6)

Ingredients
1 rooster, weighting 1 ½ kg
2 water glasses rice (not granular)
2 tbsp. butter made of staka
salt
6 water glasses of the meat's broth
1/4 water glass lemon juice

Preparation
Put the cock in a saucepan half-full with water. Add salt
and boil it for about 1 hour. When it is ready, take it
out of the saucepan and strain it.

For the pilaff: Put 6 water glasses of broth in a
saucepan (if it is not enough, add some water).
When it comes to the boil, add the rice, stirring
continuously in order for the food not to stick.
Cook for about 20 minutes (until there is no more
broth left). A few minutes before the rice is ready,
you can add ½ water glass lemon juice if you want.
When the food is ready, remove the saucepan from
the fire, sizzle the butter in a coffee-pot, pour it over
the pilaff and mix well. Leave it covered for 2 minutes and it is ready to be served.

Braised rooster (either with okra or spaghetti) (serves 6)

Ingredients
1 rooster, weighting 1 ½ kg
3 large ripe tomatoes, grated
1 onion, finely chopped
3/4 water glass, olive oil
½ water glass red wine
salt, pepper
½ kg okra or ½ kg spaghetti

Preparation
Wash the rooster and cut it into portions. Put the oil in a saucepan, brown the onion for 3 minutes and then add the cock and brown it. Add salt, pepper and the wine and when the food comes to the boil (after 2-3 minutes), add the tomatoes and cook at normal heat for about 40'. If needed, add some water. If you want to cook the cock with okras or spaghetti, after ½ hour add the okras -which you have cleaned and washed- (or the spaghetti) and continue cooking the food at normal heat for 20 minutes (or 10 minutes if you have used spaghetti). If needed add some extra water.

Pigeons (palazakia) with crushed olives (serves 6)

Ingredients
6 pigeons cut in four
1 large onion, finely chopped
2 - 3 ripe tomatoes
3/4 water glass, olive oil
salt, pepper
100 gr. crushed olives

Preparation
Put the oil in a saucepan. When it starts to sizzle add the onion and brown it. Add the pigeons, salt and pepper and cook for 5-6 minutes. Then add the tomatoes and some water, if needed, and cook the food for 40-45 minutes. 3 minutes before the food is ready, add the olives and bring them to the boil.

Thrushes with omelette (serves 4)

Ingredients
6 thrushes
6 eggs
½ water glass, olive oil
salt, pepper, oregano

Preparation
Cut the birds in four. Add salt and pepper, sprinkle with some oregano and fry them in sizzling oil on both sides, for 10 minutes. Then beat the eggs, add them in the pan and continue cooking for 2 minutes.

Pigeons (Palazakia) casserole (Stifado)
(serves 4)

Ingredients

4 pigeons
½ kg small onions (for stew)
2/3 water glass, olive oil
1 water glass, white whine
1 water glass, red wine
2 ripe tomatoes
1 tsp. vinegar
bay, clove, thyme
salt, pepper

Preparation

Wash and cut the pigeons in half.
Brown them in the oil on both sides
(for 5 minutes), add the onions, salt
and pepper and 3 minutes later, add the
white wine. 35 minutes later, add the
flavourings and bring the food to the
boil. If needed, add a bit of water.
This food can also be prepared with red
sauce. In that case, add red wine in it.
Add 2 finely chopped ripe tomatoes
after having added the onions, and a
tsp. vinegar just before adding the
flavourings.

Beverages - Desserts

Beverages

Malotira

Malotira or Malothira, of the family of Labiatae. It is a mossy, bushy and brush-wood-like plant that grows in mountain areas. Dioskouridis describes three different kinds of this plant, the first one is named Iraklia. You can drink it as a tisane, with some honey or combined with other herbs (sage, dittany).

Rosemary (Dentrolivano)

It is called rosemary, its' Latin name is Rosmarinus officiualis, and belongs to the family of Labiatae. The Romans named it "Rosmarinum". It is an evergreen plant, bushy, of dark green colour, with dense, very thin, lance-shaped leaves that have a very pleasant scent. It is self-sown, grows all over Crete and has been known in Greece since antiquity. It is used fresh or dry, in sauces made for seafood and fish, when cooking roast or grilled meat, boiled lamb, chickens, mushrooms and salads, and mainly as a beverage. It is also being used in the pharmaceutical industry since it also has healing properties (stimulating properties, insomnia, indigestion, alopecia, hysteria, and cellulite). It also favours apiculture.

Sage (Faskomilo)

Latin name: Salvia officiualis L., of the Labiatae family. It mainly is a self-sown bush, with lance-shaped, saw-like, woolly leaves, which have an ashen-green colour and strong scent. It flowers in the end of spring and its' flowers are whitish and cluster-shaped. The word itself (sfakos + milea) is of ancient origin. Dioskouridis names it "Elelisfakon" and the Latins "sacred plant" (herba sacra) because they considered it to be a very good medicine for several ailments (period disorders, fever, cramps). It is mainly used as a beverage, either alone or with malotira and dittany. It is mostly picked between May and September. It is also used when cooking braised meat, red sauces or vegetable dishes (add only 1-2 leaves as it has a very strong scent). It is a pharmaceutical herb and warming tisane and when distilled, it produces an essential oil useful in pharmaceutics and soap making.

Dictamo

Latin name: Origanum dictamus of the family of Labiatae. The ancient Greeks named it "artemidion", since it was Artemis' (Diana's) gift to them, so as to cure the wounds that she sometimes carelessly inflicted with her arrows. It is one of the most important healing herbs of antiquity - the plant named "diktamnon" of the Dikti mountains - since it was considered to be the cure for most illnesses. An indigenous plant of Crete. The words diktamo or erontas, stamato-horto, livanohorto, malliarohorto and many other synonyms are being used to name this rare aromatic plant that only grows in Crete. It is a perennial, self-sown moss and has 3 variations, according to the size of its' leaves: narrow-leafed, broad-leafed and medium-leafed.

The Dittany is a branchy plant, with slightly thick leaves that have dense white hair. Its' flowers are rosy and have a very nice scent. It endures the drought, which is why it can be mainly found in barren, rocky areas. It usually grows in great heights and steep cliffs. It is being used as a tisane, either alone or with sage and malotira. 2 or 3 leaves are enough for 1 cup, more of them would make the tisane slightly bitter. It is a stimulating and refreshing tisane, ideal for cold winter nights. It has stimulating and healing properties. Erontas is being used to make a stimulating drink. Put 30 gr. of this herb in 1 litre of white wine, soak it for 2 weeks, and drink 1 water glass of the mixture daily, for 1 week. Avoid long-term use. Pregnant women should not use it since it has abortive properties.

Orgeat from Chania (Soumada)

It is one of Crete's traditional liqueurs. Yet nowadays, it is also being produced in other areas of Greece. It is a thick liqueur of whitish colour that is made of bitter almonds' juice and sugar syrup. It is being consumed in winter, thinned down with hot water and some cinnamon. It is a particularly stimulating tisane.

Its' name derives from an Indian dialect: souia = a kind of drink. It used to be a homemade product, yet nowadays, it is also produced by small refreshment industries of the Chania Prefecture. It is prepared in the following way: pound the almonds well and boil them in some water, until they turn into mash. Then add sugar syrup, some rosewater and some bitter almond emulsion. Mix well until the mixture turns into a somewhat thick mash.

Desserts - Sweets

Xerotigana (a)

Ingredients:

For the dough
1 kg all purpose flour
1 egg
½ water glass milk
1/4 water glass, tsikoudia
oil (for frying)
For the syrup
2 tbsp. honey
1 water glass sugar
sesame (optional)
1 glass of water cinnamon

Preparation

Put the flour in a big bowl, add some water, the egg, milk and tsikoudia and knead until the dough becomes hard. Let it rise for 1-2 hours. Then roll out a very thin pastry sheet, cut it in stripes (2-4 cm), fold it in various shapes and fry the xerotigana in sizzling oil *. See that their colour turns golden and not brown. When they are ready, take them out of the pan and strain them. Then prepare the syrup (for 10-15 xerotigana) as follows: Mix the water and sugar in a saucepan stirring continuously, and let it boil for 10-15 minutes until the syrup becomes thick. Remove from the fire, add the honey and continue stirring in order for the syrup not to stick. Then dip the xerotigana in it one by one, soak them for 1-2 minutes, take them out, put them in a large flat dish and sprinkle with some sugar, cinnamon and some burnt sesame, if you want.
Use plenty of oil during frying because the xerotigana must be floating in it.

Xerotigana (b)

Ingredients

3 eggs
the juice of ½ lemon
oil
salt
flour (for all uses), as much as it takes
water

Preparation

There is another version for the preparation of the dough:
Beat the eggs, lemon juice, oil and salt together and when they have become a smooth mixture, add the flour and water and continue kneading.
The rest of the procedure is the same as in "Xerotigana (a')".

Samousades
(20-30 pieces)

Ingredients
150 gr. nuts
150 gr. almonds
30 gr. sesame
½ tsp. cinnamon
½ kg all purpose flour (for the pastry sheet)
syrup

Preparation
Pound the nuts and almonds in a mortar. Put them in a bowl, add the sesame and cinnamon and mix them. Roll out a pastry sheet, like you do for the Kalitsounia, fill each piece with a spoonful of the mixture, roll them up and put them in the oven for 20-25 minutes, at 180° C. Then pour syrup over them and serve.

Koutalites
(15-20 pieces)

Ingredients
1/4 kg all purpose flour
water
honey or petimezi (grape-juice syrup)

Preparation
Put the flour and water in a big bowl and mix them with a spoon until they become a thick mash. Put oil in a frying pan and when it gets sizzling hot, pour spoonfuls of the mixture in it and fry until the koutalites brown on both sides. Then pour honey or petimezi over them.

Avgokalamara

Ingredients
1 kg all purpose flour
3 eggs
1/4 water glass, olive oil
syrup (6 glasses of water, 3 water glasses sugar,
boil until it thickens)
200 gr. nuts, finely chopped
200 gr. almonds, finely chopped
1 tbsp. sesame
water*

Preparation
Mix the eggs in a big bowl, add the oil,
water and flour and knead until the dough
becomes hard. Leave it rise for 1-2 hours.
Roll out a very thin pastry sheet, cut it in
stripes (10-15 cm), roll them around a fork
and fry them in sizzling oil until their colour
turns golden. Take them out of the pan and
strain them. Then pour some syrup over
them (you can add some honey in it) and
sprinkle with the nuts, almonds and sesame.
* enough for the dough to become hard

Halvas

Ingredients

1/4 water glass margarine or fresh butter
1 water glasses semolina
200 gr. shelled almonds, roughly chopped
1 water glasses sugar
8 glasses of water
some cinnamon
some clove

Preparation

Put the margarine (or fresh butter) in a saucepan. When it melts, add the semolina, stir for 2-3 minutes until it browns and then add the almonds.

Put the water and sugar in another saucepan. When it boils, mix with the semolina, add the cinnamon and clove and boil them for about 15-20 minutes, stirring from time to time, until the mixture absorbs all the syrup. Then leave the Halvas to cool and pour it in a form. When you take it out of the form, sprinkle with some cinnamon.

Halvas with sesame

Ingredients

640 gr. honey
640 gr. sesame
½ glass of water
1 orange peel
some nuts

Preparation

Put all the ingredients in a saucepan and cook them until the mixture becomes thick, stirring continuously in order for it not to stick. If you want to check whether it is ready, make a small ball using a bit of the mixture and throw it on something. If it does not break, it is ready. Then put the mixture in a wet wooden surface, in order for it not to stick and using a small stick, which you will sprinkle with rosewater from time to time, roll the mixture out and cut it in pieces.

Halvas with citrons

Ingredients

1 ½ kg citrons
vanilla
1 kg sugar
shelled almonds, browned and cut in four
½ kg honey
1 soup plate nuts, cut in four
rosewater

Preparation

Scrape the citrons, cut them in pieces and
boil them. When they are ready, strain
them, put them in a saucepan, add ½ glass
of water, the sugar, honey and vanilla and
boil them until their water evaporates.
Add the nuts, almonds and rosewater and
mix well. Put the Halvas in a form and
when it dries, put it in a large flat dish and
sprinkle with sugar.
You can also make the Halvas as follows:
use the mixture to make longish pieces,
roll them in glazing sugar and serve them
in a large flat dish.
*If the citrons are overcooked while boil-
ing, make a syrup using sugar, honey and
320 gr. water and when it thickens, add
the citrons to it.

Moustalevria

Ingredients
2 ½ kg must
1 tsp. ash
1 water glass all purpose flour
1 tbsp. corn-flour
cinnamon
250 gr. nuts, roughly pounded
100 gr. sesame

Preparation
Put the must in a saucepan. When it gets warm, add the ash and boil the mixture for about 1 hour, skimming it often. Let it cool and strain it. Take 4 water glasses of the strained must and put it in another pan. When it gets warm, take half of it, put it in another pan and mix with the flour and corn flour. When the rest of the must boils, add the flour and corn flour mixture in it slowly, stirring continuously. Add some cinnamon and pepper. When the mixture thickens, remove it from the fire, add the nuts and mix. Put the mixture in small bowls and sprinkle with some cinnamon and sesame.

Galaktoboureko*

Ingredients
7-8 cups fresh milk
2 cups sugar
1 cup semolina
6 eggs
½ cup butter
Vanilla flavour, a little rose water
½ kilo phyllo pastry

For the syrup:
4 cups water
2 cups sugar
1 lemon rind for flavouring

Preparation
Pour the milk in a pot, bring to boil and then add the sugar. Remove from heat, add the rose water, the vanilla, the semolina little-by-little while constantly stirring, until all ingredients are dissolved. Return the pot to the heat, add the eggs one by one while constantly stirring, so as the cream does not stick to the bottom and sides of the pot. As soon as the cream thickens, remove from heat and allow to cool. Layer the pastry sheets (8-10 sheets) on a baking pan and brush them with butter. Then spread the cream on top and cover it with the rest of the buttered pastry sheets. Use a knife to score the top in pieces and bake at 180oC for 40-45 minutes.

Syrup
Place all ingredients for the syrup in a skillet and simmer until the sugar is completely dissolved (about 10 minutes). Pour the syrup over the pie.

* Galaktoboureko: Milk pie made with a semolina cream, phyllo pastry and honey

Patouda

For the dough
3 glasses Cretan olive oil
1 glass sugar
1 glass milk
1/2 tsikoudia
2 tsp. ammonia
2 eggs
1/3 glass of aloussia (produced by boiling water with a teaspoon ash and then draining it)

For the filling:
1/2 glass water
1 tsp. nutmeg
1 kg. walnut and almond chest
1 glass sugar
1 glass honey
2 glasses ground sesame

Preparation
Knead a dough with the aforementioned ingredients. For the filling, first make a syrup with the water, sugar and honey and when it is ready, stir in the remaining ingredients. Take a small piece of dough (the size of an apricot), make it round, open it slightly in the middle, fill it with a tbsp. of the filling and close it again. Bake them until they brown and when they have cooked sprinkle with finely ground sugar.

Quinces (whole)

Ingredients
9 whole quinces
10 tsp. honey
10 tsp. sugar
cinnamon
200 gr. ground almonds
200 gr. nuts, pounded
cloves
1 slice of bread, grilled
250 gr. rosewater

Preparation
Peel the 9 quinces and boil them in water, having stuffed each one of them with 1 tsp. honey, 1 tbsp. sugar and cinnamon. Prepare the filling as follows: put the almonds, some nuts, 1 tbsp. sugar, the cinnamon, cloves and the slice of bread in a saucepan, add some water and cook them for a while. When the quinces are ready, stuff them with the filling and then boil them in their own syrup, adding some honey and sugar. Then sprinkle with plenty of rosewater, roll them in sugar and your quinces are ready.

Grapes preserve

Ingredients

1 kilo grapes
1 kilo sugar
2-3 leaves apple geranium leaves

Preparation

Cut the stems from the grape and select the ripe and firm ones. Wash them well and place them in a pot with sugar. Boil over low heat, until the sugar dissolves and turns syrupy. Add the geranium leaves and simmer.

* Fruit preserves: In Greece fruits are preserved in syrup and are traditionally served as a candy on a spoon along with coffee.

Loukoumades*

Ingredients

For the dough:
2 cups water
2 cups flour
2 cups olive oil
1 teaspoon salt
2 teaspoons baking soda
3 eggs
3 cinnamon sticks
For the syrup:
2 cups sugar
1 cup water
2 teaspoons honey
2-3 tablespoons lemon juice

Preparation

Place water, salt, baking soda, oil and cinnamon in a deep pan and boil for 2-3 minutes. Then slowly pour in the flour and stir constantly, until the mixture becomes uniform. Remove the pan from the fire, let it cool down for 10-15 minutes and add the eggs one by one, while stirring constantly.

Then, heat the olive oil in a deep frying pan. Use a clean spoon to take small balls of dough from the prepared mixture and place them into the heated oil. Fry them until golden brown and take them out with a perforated skimmer.

Syrup

Combine all ingredients for the syrup in a pot and boil for 5 minutes. Remove from heat, immerse the loukoumades into the pot and let them soak. Afterwards, place them on a platter and sprinkle with sesame and cinnamon.

* Loukoumades: Ball-like doughnuts in the size of a tablespoonful, which are deep-fried in hot oil and soaked in honey syrup.

Walnut biscuits

Ingredients

3 cups walnuts
1 cup breadcrumb
5 eggs
1 ½ small cup cognac
2 ½ cups sugar
1 teaspoon baking soda
1 teaspoon cinnamon and powdered cloves
Icing sugar

Preparation

Beat the egg yolks with the sugar in a large bowl. Beat the egg whites until fluffy and add them to the mixture. Stir in the breadcrumbs, the dissolved baking soda, the cognac, the cinnamon, the cloves and the walnuts. Mix all ingredients very well and then use the mixture to form oval shaped biscuits. Butter a baking sheet, arrange the biscuits and bake them for 15 minutes, at 180oC. Sprinkle them with cognac, sprinkle with icing sugar and serve.

Olive oil biscuits

Ingredients

3 cups olive oil
2 cups sugar
2 cups cinnamon, boiled
1 packet baking powder
½ packet baking ammonia
Approx. 2 kilos flour, all purpose
Sesame

Preparation

Combine the olive oil with the sugar in a large bowl and mix well for 5 minutes. Add the rest of the ingredients and the flour. Knead the mixture well into pliable dough. Form small biscuits, place them on a baking pan and sprinkle with sesame. Bake in the oven for 20 minutes, at 180oC.

Kourabiedes

Ingredients

2 cups fresh butter
4-5 cups flour
½ cup sugar
2 egg yolks
1 teaspoon baking powder
1 teaspoon vanilla powder
A little rose water
500gr icing sugar

Preparation

In a bowl beat the butter until frothy. Add the sugar, the egg yolks and keep on beating vigorously. Combine the flour with the baking powder and the vanilla flavour and gradually blend it into the mixture. Beat thoroughly into a uniform, thick dough. Shape pieces of dough into flat balls or crescents and place them onto a baking pan. Bake for 15-20 minutes, at 180oC. Remove from the oven, sprinkle with rose water, dredgewith icing sugar and serve.

* Kourabiedes: Traditional Christmas biscuits dredged with plenty confectioner's sugar.

Melomakarona

Ingredients

2 cups olive oil
1 ½ cups sugar
2 tablespoons cinnamon and powdered cloves
1 cup orange juice
2 teaspoons baking soda
1 teaspoon baking powder
Flour, as much as it takes to make an elastic dough
For the syrup:
2 cups sugar
2 cups honey
1 cup water
1 small cinnamon stick
walnut, finely chopped

Preparation

Beat the olive oil with the sugar, until you obtain a uniform mixture. Dissolve the baking soda, cinnamon, cloves, and baking powder in the orange juice and blend in. Add the flour gradually to the mixture and work constantly into a uniform, soft dough. Roll and shape small pieces of dough into oval shaped biscuits and flatten them with the palm of your hand. Place them on a baking sheet and bake for 30-35 minutes, at 180oC. In a skillet boil the syrup (see recipe for loukoumades). Dip the melomakarona into the hot syrup and let them soak for 1-2 minutes. Then, place them on a platter and sprinkle with sesame and finely chopped walnuts.

* Melomakarona: Traditional Christmas oval-shaped biscuits soaked in honey syrup.

Halvas with yoghurt

Ingredients
1 small cup yoghurt
1 small cup sugar
1/4 water glass milk
2 small cups semolina (or 1 small cup
semolina and 1 small cup flour)
80 gr. whitened almond kernel, pounded
1 tsp. soda
2 sachets of vanilla
some lemon juice

Preparation
Beat the yoghurt and sugar well and then
slowly add the semolina until it is absorbed
by the mixture. Add the almonds and
vanilla and thin the mixture down with the
milk (slightly lukewarm).
Dissolve the soda in the juice of ½ a lemon
and add it in the mixture. Line a small
baking pan with oil or butter, sprinkle
some semolina in it and pour in the mixture. Cover the pan with a greaseproof
paper and put it in the oven, at 200° C.
When the Halvas is ready, carve it in
pieces and pour boiling hot syrup on it,
made of 1 small cup of sugar and 1 small
cup of water.

Sweet orange sticks

Ingredients
5 oranges with thick peel
2 lemons with thick peel
1 kg sugar (more or less)*
1/4 water glass water

Preparation
Slightly scrape the oranges and lemons
(only to remove their colour). Peel them,
and cut the peels in small, thin sticks. Boil
the sticks for 1-2 minutes (in order to soak
out the bitterness), strain them and put
them in a big bowl filled with water. Soak
them for 24 hours, changing the water 2-3
times. Then strain them again, add the
sugar and water, boil them until all the
water evaporates and strain them once
more. Roll them in sugar and put them in
the oven for 1 hour, at 100° C.
* 1 kg of sugar goes for every 100 pieces.

Easter Cookies

Ingredients
1280 gr. all purpose flour
75 gr. butter
1 water glass milk
6 eggs
2 water glasses sugar
10 gr. ammonia
1-2 egg yolk (for basting the rolls)

Preparation
Put the butter and sugar inside a big bowl
and beat them until the mixture becomes
white and smooth. Beat the egg whites and
egg yolks (add some sugar) in two different bowls, until they turn into meringue.
Dissolve the ammonia in the milk. Add
the egg whites, egg yolks and milk in the
butter-sugar mixture. Finally, add the flour
- as much as it needs. Use the dough to
make rolls in the shape of a stick or an S
and glaze them with egg yolk (or sprinkle
with sugar). Cover the baking pan with
greaseproof paper, put the rolls on it and
bake them in the oven at 170°C, for about
½ hour (until they brown).

Sweet with pumpkin

Ingredients
1 kg pumpkin
1 water glass, sugar
cinnamon
1/4 water glass, milk
pastry sheet (for the baking pan)

Preparation
Grate the pumpkin, squeeze out its' liquids and add the sugar and cinnamon. Then roll out two pastry sheets. Take one of them, glaze it with oil on both sides, lay it in the baking pan, pour the mixture over it and cover with the other pastry sheet. Pour the milk over the sweet and put it in the oven for 1 hour, at 180° C.

Sweet with despoles (medlars)

Ingredients
2 ½ kg medlars
more than 1300 gr. sugar
1 glass of water, not full
vanilla
1 lemon

Preparation
Clean the medlars, remove their skin and seeds and put all the ingredients in a saucepan. Put 1 water glass sugar for every 3 water glasses of medlars. Boil them for about 20 minutes, adding some vanilla for flavour. Remove the pan from the fire and leave the medlars rest for a day, covered with a sieve or a thin towel (do not cover them with the pan's lid). The following day, put the saucepan on the fire, add the lemon juice and boil the medlars until their syrup thickens (about 20 minutes).
If you want to check whether the syrup is thick enough, trickle a drop of it on a surface. If the drop does not roll off that spot, the syrup is ready.

© Editions "Mystis"
Antonis Tsintaris & Co.

71500 Heraklion, Menelaou Parlama 108str.
Tel.: 2810 – 346451- Fax: 2810 221908
info@mystis.gr – www.mystis.gr